W*NKER
NOMICS

W*NKER NOMICS

A DEEP-DIVE INTO WORKPLACE BULLSH*TTERY

James Schloeffel
& Charles Firth

Hardie Grant

BOOKS

FOR AMERICAN READERS

While Australian and British readers will be familiar with the term wanker, for our North American readers, an explanation may be required.

Imagine someone who lacks self-awareness, vastly overestimates how interested strangers are in their work, and whose self-confidence significantly outstrips their abilities. Sorry, you live in America – that's not helping you narrow it down is it?

Okay, imagine that guy in your workplace – let's call him Chad – who uses words like 'circle back' and 'synergise', and wants to 'quickly jump on a call to ideate some killer strategies' before his 'hard stop' at 3.30 pm, and says sorry he has to 'take this call' because he's 'closing an important deal'. He's a wanker.

In America, you might call this type of person a jerk, jackass or 'someone who trades crypto'. We call them wankers.

CONTENTS

Introduction 8
Safety induction 12

UNIT 1:
How to talk like a wanker 15

UNIT 2:
Small talk 83

UNIT 3:
Securing a new job 99

UNIT 4:
Collaboration 115

UNIT 5:
Meetings 127

UNIT 6:
The purpose of HR 165

UNIT 7:
LinkedIn 169

UNIT 8:
Using email 191

UNIT 9:
How to be a manager 201

UNIT 10:
Starting your own corporation 211

Next steps 251

About the authors 254

PICTURE THIS. YOU'RE SITTING IN A MEETING AT WORK. YOUR COLLEAGUES ARE DEEP IN SERIOUS DISCUSSION. BROWS ARE KNITTED, HEADS ARE NODDING. WHITEBOARDS ARE GROANING UNDER THE WEIGHT OF IMPORTANT-LOOKING VENN DIAGRAMS AND COLOURFUL POST-IT NOTES.

Terry says he wants an end-to-end, digital-first solution by COB Friday.

Fiona says she'll have to take that offline and circle back later.

Samantha apologises for having a hard stop but promises to socialise the deck before close of play.

Arjan suggests putting a pin in it.

And then quite suddenly, out of the blue, you catch yourself thinking, 'Hang on … what the fuck are they talking about?' Like, seriously, what do those words even mean?

What is an end-to-end solution? Does Terry even know?

Was there a reason Arjan just said the word 'ideate' instead of 'think'?

And why did Janet – a 50-year-old accountant who has never shown any discernible interest in sport – just use a baseball analogy to describe her profit-and-loss statement?

As Terry reiterates the need for outcomes-focused, customer-centric, reimagined paradigms, two important questions emerge. One: 'Has everyone gone insane?' and two: 'Have I been unwittingly inducted into a cult, or worse, onboarded into a cult?'

The answer to those two questions is yes and sort of (the preferred term is 'Values-driven, strategically aligned team' rather than 'cult').

But terminology aside, what is increasingly apparent to you is that you are trapped inside a vertically integrated, 360-degree bullshit-making machine.

There is good news and bad news.

The good news is that, unlike a religious cult, you can leave at any time and go work somewhere else. The bad news is that your new workplace will also be filled with agile, best-practice twats wanting to align their Purpose Statement to your human capital moving forward.

In other words, the wank is inescapable. Like an outbreak of chlamydia in a college dorm room, it's everywhere. And unfortunately no-one seems to be working on a vaccine.

It's in boardrooms, lunch-rooms and Microsoft Teams break-out rooms. In banks, schools, councils, day-care centres, government departments, university faculties, and beauty salons.

It's in LinkedIn posts, all-staff emails, job ads, OH&S policies and the Mission Statements that ladder up to Purpose Statements to align with Values and Vision Statements that are designed to achieve best-practice outcomes going forward.

Because the truth is, you simply won't last in today's working world if you can't get aligned with your company's meaningless new Core Values or use the phrase 'I am maxed out from a bandwidth perspective right now.'

Are we saying that you have no choice but to suck it up and surrender to the utter bullshittery of the modern working world?

No, of course not. What we're saying is, you should lean into the new paradigm and grasp the opportunity with both hands, which basically means the same thing but sounds more impressive.

Because the truth is, you simply won't last in today's working world if you can't get aligned with your company's meaningless new Core Values or use the phrase 'I am maxed out from a bandwidth perspective right now.' You'll continue to get overlooked for promotions, pay rises and $50 gift cards in recognition of your performance if you can't synergise the learnings from the OMT WIP into a set of actionable deliverables.

The only smart choice, in fact the only choice at all, is to become a wanker yourself. And that's where this book comes in. On the following pages you'll find the tools to not just survive, but thrive, in the working world. From talking like a wanker in the office to posting like a wanker on LinkedIn, as well as navigating useless meetings and mastering the art of passive-aggressive emails, you'll learn how to outmanoeuvre your colleagues and optimise your outcomes. Moving forward.

Ready to get started? Great! Well, let's not waste any more time. Let's get you onboarded ...

SAFETY INDUCTION

Before progressing any further in this book, it is essential that you pretend to read this safety induction and then tick the box below.

~~At Wankernomics, your safety is our first priority.~~ [Actually, that's not quite true. If we're being totally honest, the number of books we sell is definitely a higher priority. Don't get us wrong, we'd prefer you didn't hurt yourself while reading this book. But if we had to choose between an injury to you – someone we've never met – and shifting a few more copies of this book, well, we hope there's good healthcare where you live.]

~~At Wankernomics, your safety is our second priority.~~ [Although, come to think of it, that's not true either. Holidays are also a higher priority, so ...]

At Wankernomics, your safety is our seventh priority. So please take a moment to read through this short safety induction.

FIRE

You may have heard of a thing called fire. Fire is bad. Catching on fire falls outside of our company Values. If there is a fire while you are reading this book, a loud alarm will sound. Please just ignore it and continue reading until someone else in the room says, 'Shit, I think it actually *is* a fire', upon which you should madly elbow your way out of the building.

LIFTING BOXES

Lifting boxes is not usually a task required while reading a parody self-help book, but we're going to talk about it anyway, because this is an induction.

If, for some incredibly unlikely reason, you are required to lift a box while reading this book, remember to bend your knees and make a small but audible grunt as you lift.

SHOWING RESPECT

Remember that it is rude to interrupt. So please, be sure to say 'Sorry to interrupt' when you interrupt someone to tell them how good this book is.

FIRST AID

Small physical injuries like paper cuts, sustained while reading this book, can be treated using a simple bandage. Unfortunately there is no remedy for the psychological trauma that comes with the realisation that you are wasting the best years of your life in a meaningless office job surrounded by people you hate. Although sucking on alcohol wipes can provide temporary relief.

☐ I have read the safety induction and agree to the 450-page terms and conditions document which can be found at www.wankernomics.com/terms_and_conditions.pagenotfound.htm.

UNIT 1:
HOW TO TALK LIKE A WANKER

THE FIRST STEP TO BECOMING A WANKER IS LEARNING HOW TO TALK LIKE ONE.

While it might be awkward at first to say 'Shall we have a quick huddle and unpack the key learnings?' to a group of adults, with time it will become second nature.

Before you know it, you'll have forgotten how to say straightforward phrases such as 'Email me the PowerPoint please' and instead instinctively say, 'Can you revert back with the deck? Thanks, you're a star!'

At last, your career will begin to take off.

A quick warning before we go any further
Some people claim that they don't need to speak like a wanker in order to survive at work, arguing that their innate talent or experience in their chosen profession will be enough to get them through.

Cute. But wrong.

The truth is, it doesn't matter how smart you are. You could have worked as a brain surgeon in your previous role. You might have a PhD in theoretical chemistry. It doesn't matter. You'll still be no match for Craig in middle management who has an omni-channel thought-leadership-ideation solution that he's cascaded to Key Stakeholders for a deep-dive. He's the one getting promoted. He's the one getting the awards and the pay rises and the invites to the boss's golfing weekends. Why? Because he can say 'Let's upscale the visibility on the

key watch-outs' with a straight face and you can't.

There's no point fighting it – you simply must learn how to speak like a complete tosser too. Or, to put it another way, speaking like a complete tosser is a key deliverable that must be actioned moving forward.

If this news comes as a shock to you, don't panic, we'll teach you everything you nee ... sorry, we'll get you upskilled on the core competencies you'll need to thrive.

Following are some key rules to adhere to when you speak at work. There's no need to rush when learning these rules – focus on mastering one rule before moving on to the next. To use a sporting analogy that allows us to pretend we're Olympic athletes and not office workers chained to our desks: this is a marathon, not a sprint.

RULE 1:

Never let on that you don't know what you're doing

The working world is entirely underpinned by people who don't know what they are doing, but who use words like symbiotic and deliverables to give the impression that they do.

With a bit of practice, you too can have the confidence to walk into a job that is way above your capability, and bullshit your way through it.

✗ **DON'T SAY:** 'I totally stuffed this up because I didn't read your email.'
✓ **DO SAY:** 'There may have been a miscommunication.'

✗ **DON'T SAY:** 'I read your email but then immediately forgot about it because I was busy planning my next holiday.'
✓ **DO SAY:** 'I don't have the numbers in front of me.'

✗ **DON'T SAY:** 'I flirted with Jenny from Finance in the lift.'
✓ **DO SAY:** 'I had a cross-functional meeting with Finance, and there were a lot of moving parts.'

DON'T SAY:

'I'm totally out of my depth and I don't know what I'm doing.'

DO SAY:

'There are a lot of moving parts.'

RULE 2:

Never use one word when three or more will do

In the 1970s, the average working week in developing countries was 37 hours. By the 2020s, it was 58 hours. Research has found that the extra 21 hours is entirely due to people using unnecessarily complex sentences to impress their colleagues.

Consider the extra time it takes to say, 'I need to establish visibility on that key document moving forward' versus 'Gimme a look'.

Then consider the number of times the average worker says an unnecessarily long sentence – approximately 5000 times per week – and you'll start to see how quickly the extra time adds up.

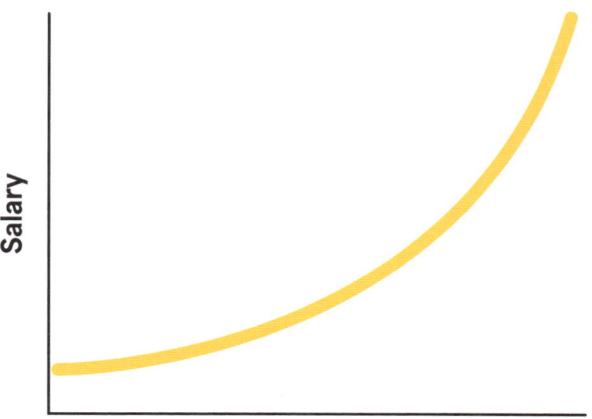

Number of words used per sentence

Unfortunately, speaking plainly and leaving work at 5 pm is not an option. Your colleagues will accuse you of slacking off or 'underachieving in relation to agreed key performance indicators'. So let your partner know you're going to be home late from now on – you're going to have to learn how to speak longer.

✗ **DON'T SAY:** 'Speak'
✓ **DO SAY:** 'Start a dialogue'

✗ **DON'T SAY:** 'Agree'
✓ **DO SAY:** 'Get into alignment' or 'get into agreement'

✗ **DON'T SAY:** 'See'
✓ **DO SAY:** 'Get a line of sight'

✗ **DON'T SAY:** 'Ask'
✓ **DO SAY:** 'Reach out'

✗ **DON'T SAY:** 'Sacked'
✓ **DO SAY:** 'Ready to embark on my next adventure'

✗ **DON'T SAY:** '   '
✓ **DO SAY:** 'Moving forward'

QUIZ
What's the difference between food and a catering solution?
Answer: About $80 per head.

DON'T SAY:

'Have you decided where to go for lunch yet?'

DO SAY:

'Just circling back on the lunch piece.'

ARE YOU GIVING 133.1%?

Before the mid-1990s, people trying their best had only ever given 100% effort to any task. But then workplace culture changed and people started giving 110% effort. This led to the awkward situation where people were devoting their entire resources and time to a given task (100%), but still falling short of the 110% baseline, thereby only actually giving 90.909% (100 as a percentage of 110).

'I'm giving 90.909%' didn't have quite the same ring to it, so people were forced to meet the 110% baseline, which was only possible to achieve by surreptitiously hiring personal assistants in India to do some of their work, which in turn caused an unexpected increase in wages in India's professional class, thereby further worsening inequality in that country.

Meanwhile, by the turn of the century, giving 110% had become normalised, and what was actually required now was to give 110% of that, which is why 'I'm giving 121%' is now the preferred terminology to use in modern workplaces. (Until, of course, that term becomes standard practice, in which case, 'I'm giving 133.1%' will become the best-in-class phrase.)

RULE 3:

MEAFA (Make Everything a Fucking Acronym)

There is something intoxicating about taking the first letters of a group of words and using them to create an acronym that no-one has ever heard before.*

Many people falsely believe that the purpose of using an acronym is to save time. But in reality, saying an acronym can actually take just as long, or longer, than SEWS (saying each word separately).

The real reason for using acronyms is to give the impression that you are more important than everyone around you.

For example, 'Let's maintain BAU processes' sounds more impressive than 'Let's maintain business-as-usual processes', which itself sounds more impressive than 'There is literally no need for me to say this sentence.'

> **DID YOU KNOW?**
> Before competitions, professional boxers will often casually use an acronym that nobody else knows. This technique has been found to boost testosterone levels by up to eighty per cent.

---

*   There is something even more intoxicating about pointing out to a colleague that in most cases the correct term is actually 'initialism', not 'acronym'.

An acronym works best when you're the only one who knows what it means, but you say it in a way that assumes everyone else knows it too. This will cause your colleagues to mistakenly think that you are more knowledgeable than them, creating a handy power imbalance that you can exploit down the track.

- ✗ **DON'T SAY:** 'My job is basically just taking coffee orders and printing out documents for dickhead senior executives.'
- ✓ **DO SAY:** 'I'm responsible for TCOs and PODs for the DSEs.'

- ✗ **DON'T SAY:** 'I've got to finish work early today so I can go to the pub.'
- ✓ **DO SAY:** 'I've got an FWE today for an urgent GTTP.'

- ✗ **DON'T SAY:** 'I'm only pretending to work today because I have a massive hangover from going to the pub yesterday.'
- ✓ **DO SAY:** 'I'm prioritising PTW today because of a mission-critical MHFGTTPY.'

EXERCISE

Translate the following into everyday English:
'The CFO needs the YTD ROI on the FY25 B2C CRM KPIs by COB.'

Answer: 'The Chief Financial Officer is a total fuckhead.'

RULE 4:

Add 'moving forward' to the end of every sentence

The terms 'moving forward' and 'going forward' were invented by a global consulting firm in the early 2000s during a project for the US government. In an unusual fee arrangement, the reasons for which are still unclear, they negotiated to be paid by the word, rather than by the hour.

In order to maximise their fee, the consultancy firm added the words 'moving forward' to the end of every sentence in meetings and reports, realising that it would have absolutely no effect on the meaning of the sentences, but a very large effect on their bottom line. The term soon caught on and now consultancy firms are worth more than US$450 billion. Of course, in a grammatical sense, 'moving forward' and 'going forward' are entirely unnecessary – everything is moving forward. It is implied. It is literally the way time works.

But for people who are in over their heads, the terms have become an invaluable tool for adding a sense of false complexity to sentences.

For example, the phrase 'We are planning to increase production' is so appallingly succinct, it's on the verge of being understandable. For all we know, you could be planning to increase production last year. 'We are planning to increase production moving forward' is much better.

✗ **DON'T SAY:** 'What is the plan for today?'
✓ **DO SAY:** 'What is the plan for today going forward?'

✗ **DON'T SAY:** 'I need to get out of the lift. Can you please move forward?'
✓ **DO SAY:** 'I need to get out of the lift. Can you please move forward, moving forward?'

✗ **DON'T SAY:** 'Hello!'
✓ **DO SAY:** 'Hello, moving forward!'

> **Adding the phrase moving forward is not always appropriate.**
> For example, if you are writing a thesis in theoretical physics about the potential existence of superluminal particles, such as positrons, which travel faster than light and therefore move backwards in time, using the phrase 'moving forward' is not required. But this is the only known exception.

Moving forward

RULE 5:

Say 'Where are you based?'

It is grossly inappropriate to ask someone where they live. Always ask them where they are based.

'Living' somewhere is old-fashioned and, frankly, a little bit embarrassing. It gives the impression that you stay in the same place every night. Being based somewhere, on the other hand, suggests you have multiple homes across the globe, one of which you've chosen to nominate as your headquarters.

Being based somewhere is especially crucial if you live somewhere shit. Casually saying 'I'm based in Milton Keynes' sounds as if you're a global citizen who has shrewdly chosen to reside in a soulless satellite town for tax reasons. 'I live in Milton Keynes' sounds like you've given up on ambition and you're ready to die.

BULLSHITTING ON THE SPOT

Making use of redundant words

Ever wondered how your higher-paid colleagues seem to answer questions effortlessly, even when put on the spot? The trick is to use words that are totally unnecessary but add to the length of a sentence. It will make it sound like you know what you're talking about, even though you definitely don't.

Piece

✗ **DON'T SAY:** 'Ahmed is looking after sales.'
✓ **DO SAY:** 'Ahmed is looking after the sales piece.'

On a quarterly basis

✗ **DON'T SAY:** 'We deliver sales results quarterly.'
✓ **DO SAY:** 'We deliver sales results on a quarterly basis.'

In this space

✗ **DON'T SAY:** 'I've done this before.'
✓ **DO SAY:** 'I have experience in this space.'

Moving forward

✗ **DON'T SAY:** 'There's a big opportunity here.'
✓ **DO SAY:** 'There's a big opportunity here moving forward.'

At the present time

✘ **DON'T SAY:** 'I don't have an update on the sales data.'
✓ **DO SAY:** 'I don't have an update on the sales data at the present time.'

Bringing it all together

'I don't have an update on that particular piece at the present time, but we'll be delivering reporting on a quarterly basis in this space moving forward.'

RULE 6:

Never take the blame

It may be tempting to take responsibility for your mistakes at work, but admitting you're at fault is very unprofessional. It smacks of honesty, integrity and 'doing the right thing' – three traits which may well form the basis of your company's Core Values (see Unit 10, page 235), but which should never be taken seriously if you want to climb the corporate ladder.

You'll do much better if you learn the language of dodging responsibility, or better yet, outright blaming another colleague.

✗ **DON'T SAY:** 'It was my fault that we didn't install new antivirus software and we've now been hacked.'
✓ **DO SAY:** 'That's more of a Terry Donaldson question.'

As well as blaming people, you can also blame technology. 'Sorry, that email was sitting in my outbox' is a wonderful catch-all that suggests it was Microsoft Outlook's fault that you have no time management skills and totally forgot a deadline.

Using the term 'living, breathing document' is handy too, suggesting that the document you were supposed to complete has been left unfinished on purpose in the spirit of agile collaboration, or some shit like that.

DON'T SAY:

'This document is only half-finished because I stayed up until 3.30 am watching Netflix and slept in.'

DO SAY:

'This is a living, breathing document.'

RULE 7:

Randomly use the word 'space'

Space is another handy word you can use when you want to make yourself, or something you're working on, sound more remarkable than it actually is.

For example, saying to someone on a Tinder date 'I'm a bank teller' is fine. But 'I work in the finance space' is much more likely to get an invite back to their place afterwards.

- ✗ **DON'T SAY:** 'I know how to use a computer.'
- ✓ **DO SAY:** 'I'm an expert in the tech space.'

- ✗ **DON'T SAY:** 'Rachel has learned how to use Instagram.'
- ✓ **DO SAY:** 'Rachel Montgomery is doing some really exciting things in the social space.'

- ✗ **DON'T SAY:** 'I am a self-trained homeopath.'
- ✓ **DO SAY:** 'I work in the healthcare space.'

- ✗ **DON'T SAY:** 'I'm an astronaut.'
- ✓ **DO SAY:** 'I work in the space space.'

'In this space'

Much like 'moving forward', the phrase 'in this space' on its own is a redundant phrase that's handy to use if you need to buy yourself time or simply increase your word count in a meeting.

- ✗ **DON'T SAY:** 'We're planning to expand our product line.' (7 words)
- ✓ **DO SAY:** 'We're planning to expand our product line in this space.' (10 words)
- ✓ **EVEN BETTER:** 'We're planning to expand our product line in this space moving forward.' (12 words)

RULE 8:

Break down the silos

Given how often the term 'silos' is bandied about these days, you could be forgiven for thinking that modern office buildings are, in fact, large storage towers filled with grain, rather than desks and chairs.

'We need to break down the silos' is intended to describe how departments have a tendency to work separately, rather than collaboratively. Unfortunately, unlike the immovable, imaginary silos, the metaphor falls over very quickly.

The idea that anyone in their right mind would willingly deconstruct a series of grain storage facilities, supposedly with the intention of then mixing together their contents, is absolutely bonkers.

The literal point of a silo is to act as a separating device from everything else around it. That's what they're for. Breaking them down would be a complete disaster. There would be grain everywhere – barley getting mixed in with the oats, wheat in with the rye, and all of it becoming wet and muddy. A year's worth of hard work down the drain. Not to mention the tricky problem of disposing of the disassembled silos, which are now taking up valuable farming land. It turns out there isn't a curb-side recycling program in place for 132-cubic-metre metal containers.

Also, maybe there's a reason why departments work separately sometimes. Just as mixing canola seeds with wheat is probably a bad idea, mixing Jennifer from Logistics with

Brittany from Marketing might be a bad idea too. Keep that shit separate.

So, yeah, whoever first came up with the phrase clearly didn't think it through.

Nevertheless, you will need to add this phrase to your arsenal if you're going to fit in. The good news is you can throw it around randomly – pretty much at any point in a conversation – and people will think you have a doctorate in organisational management.

> **YOUR BOSS:** Any ideas for increasing sales in the next financial year?
>
> **YOU:** Well, before we do anything, we need to break down the silos.
>
> **EVERYONE:** Yes, great point.
>
> So true.
>
> Brilliant!
>
> Let's document that.
>
> Love that.
>
> This guy is a genius!

Given the high regard in which breaking down silos is held, you should refer as often as possible to the times you have done it, which can basically be any time you've interacted with someone from another department.

✗ **DON'T SAY:** 'I had a brief chat to Jenny from Customer Service in the hallway.'
✓ **DO SAY:** 'I have been breaking down interdepartmental silos.'

✗ **DON'T SAY:** 'I am having an affair with Igor from Operations.'
✓ **DO SAY:** 'I am breaking down the silos between the Marketing and Operations teams.'

✗ **DON'T SAY:** 'I demolished some old grain bins that were rusted beyond repair.'
✓ **DO SAY:** 'I literally broke down the silos.'

EXPERT INSIGHT

'As a Senior Executive in the corporate space, my success has been built around using value-added, results-focused, outcomes-centred, solution-led, values-aligned hyphenated adjectives to make sentences that at first seem important but then just trail off at …'

Richard Bennington
Senior Executive

RULE 9:

Say 'Stakeholders' a lot

Stakeholders, and particularly Key Stakeholders, have a revered status within organisations. People can rarely pinpoint exactly who or what they are, except that they are inexplicably influential. Absolutely nothing can begin until they are consulted, nothing can progress without their feedback, nothing can continue until they are aligned and nothing can be completed without their buy-in.

This is useful to you because it means you can casually drop the word Stakeholders into a conversation and no-one will be able to disagree with you.

✗ **DON'T SAY:** 'I haven't done that work yet because I'm actually incredibly lazy.'

✓ **DO SAY:** 'I'm waiting for Stakeholder feedback to make sure they are aligned before moving forward on this one.'

Different types of Stakeholders
- **INTERNAL STAKEHOLDER:** A very specific jaded employee who has been at the organisation for 25 years and won't allow a project to proceed until they are placated.
- **COMMUNITY STAKEHOLDERS:** Common in development or mining projects, these are the annoying people who don't see the value of having an open-cut mine next to their house.
- **SHAREHOLDER STAKEHOLDERS:** The most important and most feared people in the world, who must be gratified at the expense of every other Stakeholder (but who are actually just 23-year-old finance graduates working at large retirement funds).
- **KEY STAKEHOLDER:** Literally anyone at all.

The word 'stakeholders' comes from the early English word 'stake-houlders'. It was commonly used by Shakespeare for its adaptability to mean anything at all. In the first draft of *Romeo and Juliet*, Juliet laments that she 'must love a loathed stake-houlder'. It was only in the final version of the script that the playwright changed the wording to 'loathed enemy'.

RULE 10:

Use the word 'lens'

There's so much talk about 'lenses' in corporations these days that it can sometimes feel like you've accidentally stumbled into a Canon camera store in the early 1990s.

Like many pieces of corporate wankery, people use the word 'lens' rather than more obvious alternatives because it lets them imagine they are involved in some sort of creative pursuit. In this case, choosing the perfect camera accessory for their next celebrity photoshoot rather than being 30 years into an unfulfilling career in accounting.

Watch carefully the next time someone at your work says, 'We need to put a customer lens on this.' You'll detect a slight shiver of excitement as they fleetingly imagine themselves at the opening of their very own photographic exhibition.

It goes without saying that if you're serious about fitting in at work, you should use the word lens as much as possible. Here are some examples to slip into your daily dialogue.

- 'Just putting a Finance lens on this for a moment ...'
- 'Let's get Julia to put a People & Culture lens on this.'
- 'Jaxxson, do you want to put a Gen Z lens on this?'

RULE 11:

Put on a hat

If playing dress-ups is more your vibe, then you can always put a hat on instead of a lens. Like putting on a lens, putting on a hat screams 'creative!' but in a more bohemian way – as if you're part of an improv troupe or a paid entertainer at an 8-year-old's birthday party. There are many ways to wear a hat:

'Just putting my design hat on here for a moment.'

'Just putting my legal hat on here for a moment.'

'Just putting my milliner hat on here for a moment.'

Be sure to make it clear that you're only putting your hat on 'for a moment' lest people get confused and wonder whether, hours later, you're still walking around the office wearing an imaginary hat.

RULE 12:

Always add value (AAV)

Whether you are adding value, value-adding or providing a value-add, increasing the amount of value is key to the value of any organisational activity.

What that value actually is, is rarely defined. 'I have a track-record for adding value for Stakeholders in this space' is an entirely acceptable sentence to use even though every single word in it is meaningless.

If *adding* value is not your thing, another acceptable option is to *create* it. Creating value, or value creation, which used to just be called 'doing your job', is an effective way to communicate to your peers what you do. Some people list 'value creation' as one of their key skills on LinkedIn, without feeling even the slightest bit embarrassed. Try it!

✗ **DON'T SAY:** 'I've been doing my job.'
✓ **DO SAY:** 'Let's touch base on the value creation piece at our next check-in.'

RULE 13:

Use the word 'key'

Whether you're talking about strategies, learnings, metrics, actions, Stakeholders, outcomes, objectives, values, performance indicators or deliverables, adding the prefix 'key' can have a transformative effect on how seriously people take you.

Use the word 'strategy' on its own and it's run-of-the-mill – something that might be used by a football team or someone trying to pick-up in a bar. But a 'key strategy' is something altogether different. It exudes importance. It has gravitas.

Tell your manager that your objective is to increase the length of your lunch breaks this year, and you can expect an official warning. Tell them increasing lunch break duration is a key objective for you (moving forward), and they'll put you on a fast-track for promotion.

The word key can also be used on its own to signify that something is business-critical without the need to provide any evidence. For example, you can say 'Stakeholder buy-in is key', 'Aligning our Purpose Statement to our Vision Statement is key', or 'Using key at the end of every sentence is key', and no-one will ever challenge you.

In fact, research has shown that you can randomly say the phrase 'Buy-in is key' at any point in a meeting, without knowing anything about the subject matter being discussed, and be assured of looking like a genius.

RULE 14:

Say 'From a perspective'

A central premise of work-talk is to avoid direct or clear language. If we all walked around saying what we meant, we'd cut our workloads in half and, as a result, many of us would be unable to justify our ongoing employment.

Framing something as being from a 'perspective' is a great way to be indirect. Why say, 'This idea will lose money,' when you can say, 'From a Finance perspective, there are some challenges with this approach'?

✗ **DON'T SAY:** 'Our customers will hate this.'
✓ **DO SAY:** 'From a consumer perspective, we may need to tweak some of the offerings.'

✗ **DON'T SAY:** 'There's no way we can do that in time.'
✓ **DO SAY:** 'It is going to be a challenge from a timeline perspective.'

ACTIVITY: MAKE UP A RANDOM PHRASE

Every workplace has that one person who is fond of using utterly ridiculous sayings and metaphors, such as 'It's like teaching elephants to dance' or 'This is like putting socks on an octopus'. They think it makes them sound interesting and quirky.

If you have a person like this at your workplace, a fun thing to do is to make up your own silly phrase and see how long it takes before they start using it too. It doesn't have to make any sense; in fact, it's better if it doesn't. It just has to be a little bit peculiar and have the sense of being profound. Here are a few to get you started:

- 'You can't build a sandcastle without sand.'
- 'If they're asking for bananas, give them monkeys.'
- 'Too many faucets, not enough taps.'
- 'It's like asking a koala to eat soup.'
- 'Let's not try to turn an armchair into a chaise lounge.'
- 'A piano only has eighty-eight keys.'
- 'You can't put a horse before the cart without feeding it first.'
- 'At the end of the day, the internet is just a series of ones and zeros.'
- 'If you do what you love, then you love what you do.'
- 'There's no "no" in "yes".'

RULE 15:

Use the word 'cascade'

It isn't enough to send a document around these days – it isn't even enough to circulate it. You need to cascade it – as if you're distributing it via that well-known document delivery device, a waterfall.

The idea of throwing bits of paper (or a digital document) into a fast-flowing body of water doesn't really work as a metaphor. But in some ways it does make sense.

Cascading (in the workplace sense) means distributing something to more junior employees – people who can probably relate to the feeling of standing at the bottom of a waterfall and getting slammed with 4000 cubic metres of water a second while they struggle to breathe.

Using 'cascade' around the office will also make you sound more senior than you are – you can't cascade something if you're at the bottom already (although, thinking about it, it's only a matter of time before some dickhead asks you to cascade something up).

Using the term also gives you an outdoorsy vibe, as if you spend your weekends trekking, rather than filling in timesheets.

✗ **DON'T SAY:** 'Can you email that to John?'
✓ **DO SAY:** 'Can you cascade those outputs to John?'
✓ **EVEN BETTER:** 'Can you cascade this up to John in SLT?'

RULE 16:

Use the word 'socialise'

There's no better example of just how far humanity has fallen than to observe the way the word 'socialise' is now used.

Socialise used to mean catching up with a group of friends for a few drinks on a Friday. Now it means sending a document to your work colleagues in a group email.

It's not just utterly depressing; the entire idea of socialising a document is patently ridiculous, as if you're taking it out after work to meet your colleagues.

> 'Hi guys, I'd like you to meet Sales Forecasts_v1.5. He's new around here so I thought I'd invite him out to meet everyone. What's that? Why doesn't he talk? Oh, that's because he's an Excel spreadsheet and he doesn't have a mouth. Good with numbers though.'

Like 'cascade' and 'loop in' and all the other jargon in this unit, you're going to need to become familiar with using the word. Sure, you might feel like an idiot asking someone to 'socialise' a document, as if it's a puppy learning how to play nicely with other dogs in a dog park. But trust us, no-one else will bat an eyelid.

✗ **DON'T SAY:** 'Has anyone else read this?'
✓ **DO SAY:** 'Has this deck been socialised with Samantha Graham's team?'

ASK WANKERNOMICS

Should I cascade this document or socialise it?

Technically speaking, you should only ever cascade a document if it has already been socialised (which should only be done once the document has been circulated). Just as you wouldn't take a dog to the dog park if you hadn't first introduced it to other dogs, you wouldn't cascade an Excel spreadsheet without first socialising it with Key Stakeholders.

So, 'Once you've circulated the document, please socialise it with the team and then cascade it to Bob Fairweather for feedback' is correct, whereas ... actually, who are we kidding, none of this makes any sense. Just use the two words liberally and interchangeably and you'll fit right in.

RULE 17:

Pretend you are back at primary school

One of the ways people try to distract themselves from the fact that they are rapidly approaching middle age while being stuck in a meaningless office job surrounded by people they despise is to pretend they're back at primary school.

Saying 'Let's jump on a call' makes it sound as if you're hanging out at the local trampoline centre, not staring at a screen while you discuss the key deliverables for Q4.

'End of play' evokes packing up your toys after spending an afternoon building Lego, neatly concealing the fact that you're actually heading off at 8 pm after finally getting through 300 unread emails.

The word 'ping' in 'ping me an email' calls to mind a computer game, making the request to send an email to a colleague about something you literally just discussed with them sound exciting.

And 'let's have a quick huddle' ... well, we'll be honest, that sounds creepy as fuck. But it's considered totally normal in many organisations, so you may as well add it to the repertoire.

✗ **DON'T SAY:** 'Call me when you're free.'
✓ **DO SAY:** 'Ping me an email before COB and we can jump on a call to discuss our next huddle.'

RULE 18:

Be outcomes-focused

It used to be implied that the reason you did something – serve a customer, write a report, install a window – was to bring about some sort of result or outcome. These days, however, you need to explicitly state that this is what you are focused on, lest people think you are suspended in a world of permanent inertia where the laws of physics do not apply.

Practise it now: 'I am outcomes-focused.'

Saying it once is not enough. You need to constantly remind people – on your LinkedIn, in performance reviews, even in casual conversation. No-one ever got demoted for saying in a meeting, 'We need to be more outcomes-focused,' even though it is essentially meaningless.

Research has shown that if you say 'I am outcomes-focused' at least three times in a job interview you will be eighty per cent more likely to secure a position well beyond your capabilities.

(For use of the word 'outcomes' in an organisational setting, see page 245.)

WHAT TO SAY WHEN SOMEONE ASKS 'HOW ARE YOU?'

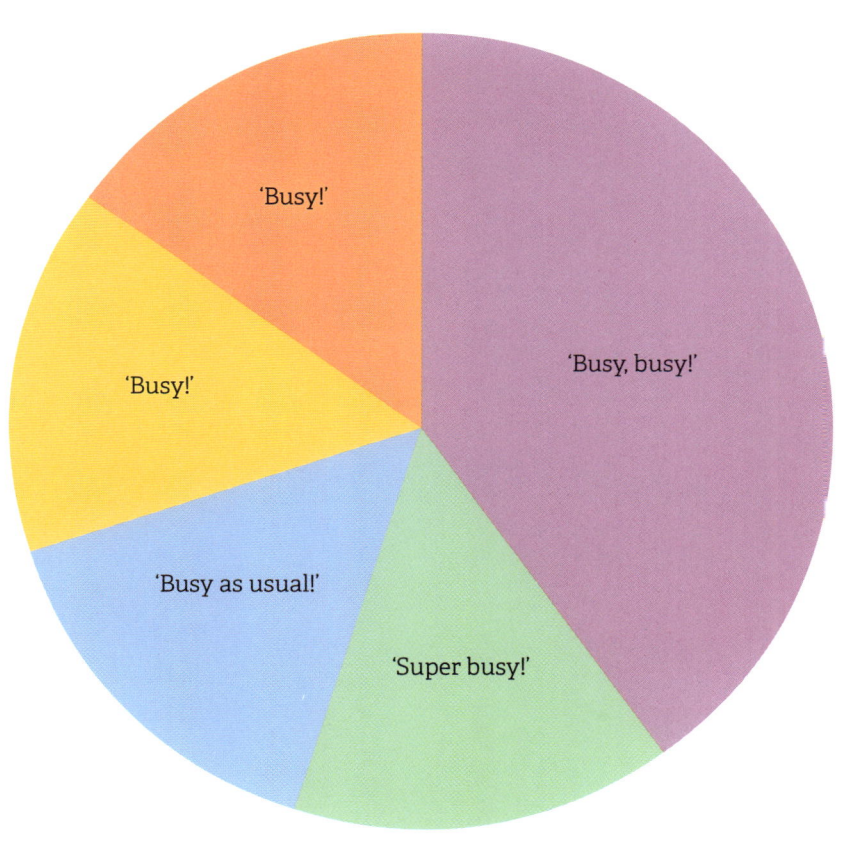

RULE 19:

Use 'ask' as a noun

'Ask' used to be a verb that meant 'to inquire'. Now it is a noun that means 'a thing that needs to be done'.

Saying 'What's the ask here?' instead of 'What do I need to do?' cleverly masks the fact that you don't know what you're doing. When paired with the word 'key', ask is particularly powerful.

✗ **DON'T SAY:** 'I have totally forgotten what the purpose of this meeting is because I was in a post-festival-induced fugue state when I set it up.'

✓ **DO SAY:** 'What's the key ask here?'

RULE 20:

Use 'watch-out' as a noun

'Watch out' used to be a warning phrase used to alert people to oncoming danger, such as in, 'Watch out! The kitchen is on fire!' These days it means basically the same thing but has been repackaged as a noun so that it sounds more professional, allowing consultants to charge you more money ('The kitchen fire is a watch-out').

As with most phrases like this, adding the word 'key' before 'watch-out' increases its potency. Come to a meeting armed with 'Three key watch-outs for the implementation delivery framework' and your colleagues will treat you like a god.

RULE 21:

Action it

If you're still using the word 'do' instead of 'action' then it's no surprise that your career is floundering. 'Action' evokes movement, excitement, superheroes, Hollywood – all of the things your workplace is almost certainly not, but would like to imagine itself to be.

✗ **DON'T SAY:** 'Can you update this please, Liam?'
✓ **DO SAY:** 'Can you action those updates please, Liam?'

✗ **DON'T SAY:** 'Whose turn is it to pick up the dog shit?'
✓ **DO SAY:** 'Whose turn is it to action the dog shit?'

✗ **DON'T SAY:** 'All done!'
✓ **DO SAY:** 'I've actioned that action!'

RULE 22:

Get into alignment

You've probably already noticed that nothing can take place in a modern organisation until everything and everyone is aligned or, better yet (if you need to increase the length of your sentence), in alignment.

Behaviours need to be aligned with the Purpose Statement, which needs to be aligned with the Strategy.

Marketing needs to be aligned with Procurement, which needs to be aligned with Stakeholders.

Everyone needs to be aligned to the Values. Prospective employees need to be aligned to the company culture.
And so on.

You can use 'aligned' to your advantage. Randomly dropping a phrase like 'Is Trish Waters aligned on this?' can turn a meeting on its head, taking the focus off the work you haven't done.

Saying 'I'm not aligned to your way of thinking' is more passive aggressive, and probably more effective than saying 'That's the worst idea I've ever heard'.

RULE 23:

Reach out

When you call or email someone, you should start the conversation by telling them that you are 'just reaching out'. This is preferred to simply saying you are 'calling them' or 'emailing them' or, God forbid, not telling them what you are doing at all and assuming they'll use the context of the situation to work it out for themselves.

'Reach out' also adds a certain loftiness to your language. 'Can you reach out to Julia in Ops?' is preferrable to 'Can you talk to Julia in Ops?' because it sounds as if you are brokering a peace deal in a warzone, rather than setting up an 11 am catch-up to discuss monthly billing processes.

RULE 24:

Use the word 'wordsmith'

Many bullshit business words stem from the user's desire to be seen as part of the creative class (see 'lens', page 42). But sometimes, people who live in smart apartments and wear a suit to work like to imagine themselves as being in touch with the working classes too. 'Wordsmith' is such an example.

'Let's get the agency to wordsmith this paragraph' evokes an image of a hardened blue-collar worker, his face smudged with coal and sweat, chiselling out sentences by hand in an open-cut mine. In reality, it's a 23-year-old junior copywriter re-wording a webpage in an air-conditioned share house in Richmond.

✗ **DON'T SAY:** 'Can you make this Mission Statement sound better?'

✓ **DO SAY:** 'Can we get the agency to wordsmith this to give it a bit more pop?'

RULE 25:

Never speak 'about' anything

Speaking 'about' something is very old-fashioned. These days you need to speak 'to' or 'around' it.

Admittedly, saying 'Jerry can speak to that slide' may make it sound as if Jerry is about to begin a one-on-one conversation with a Microsoft PowerPoint presentation, but unfortunately that's how you need to talk these days.

- ✗ **DON'T SAY:** 'OMG can we talk about how shit the new grad is?'
- ✓ **DO SAY:** 'We need to have a conversation around Bridget's under-performance.'

- ✗ **DON'T SAY:** 'Tam can explain the effect of cutting prices.'
- ✓ **DO SAY:** 'Tam can speak to the financial implications of cost-reduction measures.'

DON'T SAY:

'I don't have the language skills to articulate what I mean.'

DO SAY:

'There's a whole piece around this.'

RULE 26:

Use baseball analogies

If you live outside of North America you have almost certainly never watched a full game of baseball. Unfortunately, it's a requirement at every workplace regardless of where you live to use baseball analogies anyway. You'll need to use terms like 'curve ball', 'left-field', 'hit it out of the park' and 'touch base' in your work conversations, in the same way that Americans definitely don't say 'He's been caught holding the ball on that one' or 'The strategy is pitching in line but just missing off'.

RULE 27:

Pretend you have a practical job

People desperately trying to shut out the thought that their entire professional existence amounts to nothing more than creating PowerPoint slides and then sitting in meetings talking about those PowerPoint slides will often use terminology from more rugged, practical professions to trick themselves into thinking they are doing something useful.

Say 'That's right in my wheelhouse' and you're suddenly a boat captain navigating a storm on the high seas. 'Drill down' on something during a meeting and you can imagine yourself on an oil rig in the Atlantic. Say 'Let's ring-fence that' and you're a farmer. 'Shall we take a deep-dive?' and you're Jacques Cousteau.

If you want to take it a step further, say you've been 'working at the coalface', cleverly equating making a few sales calls last week to working with your bare hands and a pickaxe in 1900s Britain.

EXAMPLE:
'Shall we take a deep-dive and then drill down on the deliverables by ring-fencing what's in our wheelhouse?'

RULE 28:

Pretend you're a computer

If wheelhouses and ring-fences are not your jam, why not pretend you're a computer? Taking ordinary words and replacing them with technology-related terms for no reason at all seems to impress all of the right people.

✗ **DON'T SAY:** 'I'm too busy, sorry.'
✓ **DO SAY:** 'I have zero bandwidth for any extra projects right now.'

✗ **DON'T SAY:** 'Let's talk about that later.'
✓ **DO SAY:** 'Shall we take that offline?'

RULE 29:

Never say 'PowerPoint document'

Always say 'deck' or 'pack'. It brings to mind a card game, as if you're sitting in a smoky Monte Carlo casino playing blackjack rather than enduring a punishing 450-slide presentation on Q4 sales forecasts.

ACTIVITY: CREATE YOUR OWN NEW PIECE OF JARGON

STEP 1: Take a noun and turn it into a verb.

- Idea → Ideate

STEP 2: Turn the new verb you've created back into a noun.

- Ideate → Ideation

STEP 3: Turn the new noun back into a verb.

- Ideation → Ideationing

STEP 4: Turn your new word into a multi-word clusterfuck.

- Ideationing → An all-hands, blue-sky ideationing session.

RULE 30:

Say 'human-centred design'

The term 'human-centred design' started popping up a few years ago in marketing and strategy circles to describe a process for creating products or services which, until that point, had been described simply as 'design'.

Using the term provides a handy reminder to those around you that the new software, retail store or dishwasher you are developing is not intended to be used by horses. (Strangely, people who design products for horses don't tend to use the term 'horse-centred design'. Although that could be just because it's really fucking obvious that if you're designing a toothbrush for a horse it needs to be suitable for a horse.)

Presented as a groundbreaking new approach, human-centred design has been proven to increase the number of words used in meetings, emails, and living, breathing documents by 200 per cent, and the cost of consulting fees by even more.

RULE 31:

Start a dialogue

Talking to someone is very run-of-the-mill these days. You should always start a dialogue. It gives the misguided impression that you are doing something of great importance, like brokering negotiations with North Korea.

✗ **DON'T SAY:** 'Can you ask Caitlyn to fix the dishwasher?'
✓ **DO SAY:** 'Can we set up a dialogue with Caitlyn Ford on the dishwasher piece please?'

---

5 HR-APPROVED WAYS TO TELL YOUR COLLEAGUE THEY'RE AN IDIOT

1. 'We may have got our wires crossed.'
2. 'It's a great start! Let's explore some other alternatives.'
3. 'Have you tried turning it off and on again?'
4. 'Let's park that idea for now!'
5. 'You're not aligning with my Values right now.'

RULE 32:

Always circle (or loop) back

Spend a day listening in on the conversations at a modern workplace and you'd be forgiven for thinking that people are in a constant state of circular motion, spinning frantically as they reply to requests from their colleagues.

Keith is circling back with the latest sales forecast for Chen, who will loop back with her thoughts tomorrow, before Ali circles back by COB Friday.

It's enough to give you vertigo. But, as you've probably already discovered, this is one of those terms that it's impossible to avoid.

✗ **DON'T SAY:** 'Have you spoken to Caitlyn yet about fixing the dishwasher?'
✓ **DO SAY:** 'Just circling back on the Caitlyn Ford dishwasher dialogue piece we discussed at Tuesday's stand-up.'

✗ **DON'T SAY:** 'Have you decided where to go for lunch yet?'
✓ **DO SAY:** 'Just circling back on the lunch piece.'

HOW WANK-WORDS SPREAD

New pieces of jargon are introduced into workplaces every day by dickheads trying to impress their colleagues. The new piece of jargon quickly spreads to others, who may at first try to fight off the term, but given weakened herd immunity will eventually succumb.

Within the space of less than a week, everyone in the office is infected with the new term, and it's only a matter of time before it spreads to other workplaces.

Quick-fire definitions

PHRASE: 'Around this'
ACTUAL MEANING: None.
WANKERNOMICS MEANING: I am not articulate enough to use specific phrases when I talk.
EXAMPLE: 'Have you spoken to Sally Walsh? There's a huge opportunity around this piece.'

PHRASE: 'Best-of-breed' (see also 'Best-in-class')
ACTUAL MEANING: The winning animal of its breed at a dog show.
WANKERNOMICS MEANING: I want to charge you more money.
EXAMPLE: 'Our end-to-end, holistic solutions are best-of-breed.'

PHRASE: 'Best practice'
ACTUAL MEANING: The correct way to do something.
WANKERNOMICS MEANING: A passive-aggressive way of saying that something could be better.
EXAMPLE: 'Your hairdo is not considered best practice.'

PHRASE: 'Cadence'
ACTUAL MEANING: A sequence of notes or chords.
WANKERNOMICS MEANING: Frequency, but using a misappropriated musical term in order to make it sound fun.
EXAMPLE: 'What sort of meeting cadence do we want to establish here, folks?'

PHRASE: 'Competency' [especially with 'Core']
ACTUAL MEANING: Thing someone is able to do.
WANKERNOMICS MEANING: A very basic skill presented as if it's a PhD-level ability.
EXAMPLE: 'One of my core competencies is digital operability.'

PHRASE: 'Deliverables'
ACTUAL MEANING: Things that need to be delivered.
WANKERNOMICS MEANING: The things that your boss/senior management specifically think need to be done.
EXAMPLE: 'I think we might be losing focus on the key deliverables for this one, Brian.'

PHRASE: 'Drill down'
ACTUAL MEANING: Extract raw materials, such as oil, using a drill.
WANKERNOMICS MEANING: Examine in further detail, but using a power tool metaphor to make your work sound more grounded in the real world than it actually is.
EXAMPLE: 'Can you drill down on that slide a little more, Jason?'

PHRASE: 'End-to-end'
ACTUAL MEANING: Extending from one end to another.
WANKERNOMICS MEANING: We want to charge you more money by making our process sound more involved than it actually is.
EXAMPLE: 'We deliver end-to-end, holistic solutions.'

PHRASE: 'Eyeballs'
ACTUAL MEANING: The round part of the eye of a vertebrate.
WANKERNOMICS MEANING: People, but said in a way to make it sound vaguely scientific, and also to double the number of entities reached.
EXAMPLE: 'This new ad should reach a lot of eyeballs.'

PHRASE: 'Guru'
ACTUAL MEANING: Expert.
WANKERNOMICS MEANING: Wanker.
EXAMPLE: 'See that guy over there in the red fedora? He's our data guru.'

PHRASE: 'Holistic'
ACTUAL MEANING: Complete.
WANKERNOMICS MEANING: Complete bullshit.
EXAMPLE: 'We deliver end-to-end, holistic solutions.'

PHRASE: 'Huddle'
ACTUAL MEANING: Gather together.
WANKERNOMICS MEANING: A long, excruciating meeting described in playground speak to make it sound appealing.
EXAMPLE: 'Shall we have a quick six-hour huddle on the FY26 objectives?'

PHRASE: 'Ideate'
ACTUAL MEANING: Think.
WANKERNOMICS MEANING: I work in Strategy.
EXAMPLE: 'Shall we jump on a Zoom to ideate some solutions real quick?'

PHRASE: 'It's on my radar'
ACTUAL MEANING: It is visible on the electronic device I use for determining the position or speed of objects.
WANKERNOMICS MEANING: I'm not going to do anything about it.
EXAMPLE: 'Thanks for reminding me about your requested pay rise, Phoebe, it's on my radar.'

PHRASE: 'Lean in'
ACTUAL MEANING: To shift one's bodyweight forward.
WANKERNOMICS MEANING: To commit to something, even if you don't want to.
EXAMPLE: 'We need to lean into the uncertainty as we restructure the headcount moving forward.'

PHRASE: 'Learning' [especially with 'Key']
ACTUAL MEANING: Thing you have learnt.
WANKERNOMICS MEANING: I really want to just say 'What have we learnt today?', but I don't want to sound like a presenter on a children's TV show.
EXAMPLE: 'What are the key learnings from today's session, everyone?'

PHRASE: 'Loop in'
ACTUAL MEANING: To connect in a circuit.
WANKERNOMICS MEANING: Unnecessarily bring someone else into a project or conversation who will almost certainly make things more difficult.
EXAMPLE: 'Let's loop in Ibrahim on the deck and get his thoughts.'

PHRASE: 'Offices'
ACTUAL MEANING: Office.
WANKERNOMICS MEANING: Office, but said in the plural form to give the impression that you work in a large, successful multinational firm and not a two-person graphic design studio in a shared suite.
EXAMPLE: 'Let's meet at our Punt Road offices to run through the ideation outputs.'

PHRASE: 'On a daily basis' *[see also 'On an annual basis', 'On a quarterly basis']*
ACTUAL MEANING: Daily.
WANKERNOMICS MEANING: Daily, but using four words instead of one.
EXAMPLE: 'I have lunch on a daily basis.'

PHRASE: 'On the same page' *[see also 'Singing from the same song/hymn sheet']*
ACTUAL MEANING: Everyone is in harmonious agreement.
WANKERNOMICS MEANING: Everyone agrees with senior management because what other choice do they have?
EXAMPLE: 'It's great to have everyone on the same page about the new team structure.'

PHRASE: 'Operability'
ACTUAL MEANING: Whether something works or not.
WANKERNOMICS MEANING: Did you know I can say six-syllable words?
EXAMPLE: 'We need to gauge the operability on this before moving forward.'

PHRASE: 'Piece'
ACTUAL MEANING: Part, component.
WANKERNOMICS MEANING: No meaning.
EXAMPLE: 'We need to make sure it aligns with the Values piece.'

PHRASE: 'Reach out'
ACTUAL MEANING: To stretch out one's arm in order to touch something.
WANKERNOMICS MEANING: A superfluous phrase that I've added because I don't know how to be direct.
EXAMPLE: 'Just thought I'd reach out to check in on the status of the pain-point analysis.'

PHRASE: 'Revert' or 'Revert back'
ACTUAL MEANING: To reply.
WANKERNOMICS MEANING: Reply to your email, but speaking as if you are a robot.
EXAMPLE: 'Please revert on the EOI by COP.'

PHRASE: 'Rock star'
ACTUAL MEANING: A member of a famous band that performs songs within the rock genre.
WANKERNOMICS MEANING: I am patronising you by equating your ability to complete a simple task with forging a career as a successful musician.
EXAMPLE: 'Thanks for re-organising the stationery cabinet, Mia. You're a rock star!'

PHRASE: 'Synergise' or 'Synergies'
ACTUAL MEANING: The result of two things coming together to create a combined effect greater than the sum of their parts.
WANKERNOMICS MEANING: Not sure, but definitely not the above.
EXAMPLE: 'We need to synergise our synergies going forward.'

PHRASE: 'Takeaway' or 'Takeout' *[especially with 'Key']*
ACTUAL MEANING: Food that is bought from a restaurant but eaten elsewhere.
WANKERNOMICS MEANING: I'm trying to make work sound fun by using a word associated with food.
EXAMPLE: 'What are your key takeaways from the OH&S session, Pam?'

PHRASE: 'Take it onboard'
ACTUAL MEANING: To consider something (e.g. feedback).
WANKERNOMICS MEANING: I will ignore it.
EXAMPLE: 'Thanks for the feedback on the deck, Meg, I'll take it onboard.'

PHRASE: 'Take offline'
ACTUAL MEANING: Disconnect from the internet.
WANKERNOMICS MEANING: This is embarrassing to discuss in front of other people, please stop talking immediately.
EXAMPLE: 'Why don't we take the conversation about my company credit card expenditure offline?'

PHRASE: 'Touch base'
ACTUAL MEANING: To make contact with a base without being tagged, in the game of baseball.
WANKERNOMICS MEANING: Catch up, in a way that makes it sound like it's quick and casual, but in reality is likely to be long and agonising.
EXAMPLE: 'Just thought I'd quickly touch base about overhauling the financial structure of the company.'

PHRASE: 'Unpack'
ACTUAL MEANING: Empty a suitcase of its belongings.
WANKERNOMICS MEANING: I'm about to explain something simple, but I want to make it sound as if I'm doing something quite complex.
EXAMPLE: 'Let's take a moment to unpack some of the underlying assumptions on the analysis.'

PHRASE: 'Utilise'
ACTUAL MEANING: Use.
WANKERNOMICS MEANING: Use, but with three syllables instead of one.
EXAMPLE: 'The new photocopier is there for you to utilise on a daily basis, moving forward.'

A non-exhaustive list of other words that we don't have space to define but that you can confidently drop into any conversation at any time

Action
Action item
Added value
Agile
Always-on
At the end of the day
Attention economy
Baked in
Balls in the air
Baseline
BAU
Behaviours
Big data
Big idea
Big shoes to fill
Bleeding edge
Blue-sky thinking
Bottom line
Bring to the table
Build
Buy-in
C-Suite
Can everyone see my screen?
Can we make the logo bigger?
Change-agent
Circle back
Circular economy
Circulate
Clarity
Coalface
COB
Connect
Connectivity

Consensus
Consumer-centric
COP
CSR
Current state
Customer journey
Customer-centric
Customer-first
Customer-oriented
Cutting edge
De-risk
Deep-dive
Deliver
Delivery
Delta
Departmental
Dial up
Dialogue
Diarise
Disrupt
Disruptive
DNA
Dotted line
Double-click
Downsize
Drive
Driver
Drop the ball
Ducks in a row
Echo
Embed
End-user
Engagement
EOP
Fast-track

Feedback
Fit-for-purpose
Follow up
Framework
Friction
Functionality
Future state
Game-changer
Gen Z
Get a read
Granular
Great to connect!
Growth hack
Happy middle ground
Headcount
Helicopter view
High level
High-level insights
High-level response
How are you placed?
Human
I'd like to add you to my professional network
Ideation
Impactful
In the weeds
In this space
Initiatives
Innovative
Insights
Integrate
Interdependency
Interfacing
Interoperability

Is this a need to have or a nice to have?
Iterate
Join the dots
Join up
Jumping off point
Just conscious of time guys
Just touching base
Keep your CV on file
Key
Key driver
Key insights
Key learnings
Key levers
Key milestones
Key objectives
Key outcomes
Key performance indicators
Key Stakeholders
Key takeaways
Key takeouts
Key watch-outs
Ladder up
Land
Landscape
Learning
Let's park that one for now
Lever
Leverage
Living, breathing document
Look and feel
Loose end
Low-hanging fruit
Make a call
Make it pop
Maximise
Measurable
Mechanism
Metrics
Mission critical
Monetise
Move the dial
Move the needle
Offline

Offsite
Onboarding
Ongoing
Optimal
Optimise
Optionality
Out-of-the-box thinking
Outcomes
Outcomes-based
Outcomes-focused
Outcomes-led
Outcomes-oriented
Outputs
Pain point
Paradigm
Piggyback
Pivot
Press go
Proactive
Push back
Push the envelope
Put a pin in it
Quick wins
Re-imagine
Realignment
Repackage
Resonate
Results-based growth
Ring-fence
Roadmap
Saleable
Scalable
Scale
Scale-down
Scale-up
Scope-creep
Seamless
Seamless integration
Seamlessly integrated
Shift the dial
Shift the needle
Siloed
Singing from the same hymn sheet
Singing from the same song sheet
Socialise
Solutions

Solutions-focused
Solutions-led
Space
Speak to
Status
Step change
Storytelling
Strategic
Symbiotic
Take a decision
Talk to
Task-focused
There's no such thing as a bad idea
Three-dimensional chess
Tissue session
Top of mind
Top-line thoughts
Touchpoint
Traction
Transparency
Up to speed
Upscale
Upskill
User journey
Value creation
Value proposition
Value-add
Value-added
Vector
Ventilate
Visibility
Watch-out
Watch-outs
Wheelhouse
Where the rubber hits the road
Win-win
WIP
Working in silos
World-class
You're on mute
Zero-in

Applying workspeak to everyday life

Just because you've knocked off from work for the day doesn't mean you have to stop talking like a wanker. Try some of these phrases with your partner or roommate the next time you see them. They'll love it!

Around the house

✗ **DON'T SAY:** 'What shall we do for dinner tonight?'
✓ **DO SAY:** 'Let's start a dialogue around creating a satiation-solution framework.'

✗ **DON'T SAY:** 'I'm going to stack the dishwasher.'
✓ **DO SAY:** 'I'm initiating an onboarding procedure for the plates and bowls.'

✗ **DON'T SAY:** 'What are you getting from the shops?'
✓ **DO SAY:** 'Please socialise the shopping list before pressing go on future purchases.'

Talking with friends

✗ **DON'T SAY:** 'Congratulations on your new baby!'
✓ **DO SAY:** 'Congratulations on your new co-creation!'

✗ **DON'T SAY:** 'We got a cat.'
✓ **DO SAY:** 'We're onboarding a new feline-based team member, please make them feel welcome.'

EXERCISE

Sharpen your skills by re-working the titles of these popular movies and TV shows as if they were named by an annoying middle-manager. We've included some suggestions to help you get started.

ORIGINAL: *When Harry Met Sally*
RE-WORKED: *When Harry Reached Out to Sally*

ORIGINAL: *Ferris Bueller's Day Off*
RE-WORKED: *Ferris Bueller's Personal Leave Day*

ORIGINAL: *Romeo & Juliet*
RE-WORKED: *Romeo Puts Some Time in the Diary for a One-On-One with Juliet*

ORIGINAL: *We Need to Talk About Kevin*
RE-WORKED: *We Need to Have a Conversation Around Kevin*

ORIGINAL: *Succession*
RE-WORKED: *Please Find Updated Org Chart Attached*

ORIGINAL: *Frozen III*
RE-WORKED: *Can Someone Please Fix the Heating in this Office?*

ORIGINAL: *Ocean's Eleven*
RE-WORKED: *Ocean's_V11.2.1_Final_USE THIS*

UNIT 2: SMALL TALK

IF YOU'RE LIKE MOST PEOPLE, YOUR DAY AT WORK WILL GENERALLY BE A SUCCESSION OF MEETINGS AND EMAILS INTERSPERSED WITH BRIEF-BUT-AWKWARD SOCIAL ENCOUNTERS WITH COLLEAGUES YOU DON'T REALLY KNOW OR LIKE.

Whether you're preparing lunch in the kitchen, riding the lift or even just heading to the toilet, modern offices are a minefield of micro interactions that are impossible to avoid.

Even when you're working remotely, you must contend with the horror of joining a Teams meeting just that little bit too early and being stuck making inane small talk with Carol from Comms about your respective plans for the weekend.

Work small talk has its own language – separate from ordinary work talk – which you will need to master if you are to thrive at work. While this style of communicating appears to have a more relaxed tone, don't be fooled. The phrasing and word choice is very specific – with a compulsory response depending on the setting. Deviate from them at your peril.

Talking about the weekend

> **YOU:** Plans for the weekend?

> **YOUR COLLEAGUE:** Just a quiet one.

> **YOUR COMPULSORY RESPONSE:** It's nice to have those once in a while.

Preparing lunch in the office kitchen

> **YOU:** Leftover curry?

> **YOUR COLLEAGUE:** Yes.

> **YOUR COMPULSORY RESPONSE:** It always tastes better the day after.*

---

* There is absolutely no evidence to suggest that this is true but you must say this phrase anyway.

Two people arrive at work wearing the same, coloured shirt

💬 **YOUR COMPULSORY RESPONSE:** I didn't get the memo!

Your colleague has just had a baby

💬 **YOUR COLLEAGUE:** My partner just had a baby boy!

💬 **YOUR COMPULSORY RESPONSE:** How much does he weigh?**

Your colleague has just arrived back from holidays

💬 **YOUR COLLEAGUE:** I had a great time in Paris.

💬 **YOUR COMPULSORY RESPONSE:** When did you get back?***

A visitor arrives at your office

💬 **YOUR COMPULSORY RESPONSE:** Did you find the place alright?****

** Even though this information is of absolutely no interest to you, you must ask this.
*** While it may be tempting to ask about the things they did on their holiday, it is mandatory to first ask about the temporal specifics of their return journey, despite the fact you have no interest in it. Your colleague will need to follow this up with the compulsory phrase, 'Feels like I never left.'
**** You must say this even though it is patently obvious they found the place alright.

LEAVING CARD BINGO

Although less common since working-from-home has increased, the oversized leaving card signed by everyone is still a frightening feature of workplace life.

The question 'Have you signed the leaving card for Trish yet?' is enough to ruin your day, especially if you hardly know who Trish is and you have absolutely nothing to say to her. There are a number of suitable generic phrases you can use, as outlined in the bingo card below. Just be sure to sign Trish's card early, before all of the phrases are taken.

BINGO

'You'll be missed'	'Future challenges'	'Exciting new chapter'
'All the best'	'Let's stay in touch'	'Pleasure to work with'
'Big shoes to fill'	'New journey'	'Huge loss'
'Exciting!'	'Won't be the same without you'	'I'm pregnant'

HOW TO SING 'HAPPY BIRTHDAY' TO A COLLEAGUE YOU VAGUELY KNOW AND THEN STAND AROUND AWKWARDLY AFTERWARDS WHILE THEY CUT THE CAKE

The main reason companies are finding it so difficult to lure employees back into the office is not because of the convenience of working from home. It's because people are trying to avoid the excruciating experience of standing in a circle while they sing 'Happy birthday' and watch someone cut a cheap cake.

If you do find yourself in one of these situations, there are a few rules you'll need to follow:

- Stare intensely at the birthday person while you sing the song to make them feel comfortable.
- Cheer at the end of the song as if you're seven.
- Shout out something hilarious like 'How many boyfriends?'
- Say 'Anything exciting planned for your birthday?'
- Pretend you have a meeting to go to and leave as soon as you're given a slice of cake.

The Wednesday problem

Making small talk is fairly straightforward on Mondays, Tuesdays, Thursdays and Fridays (see illustration below). Wednesdays, however, are a problem. Too much time has passed since the previous weekend to enquire what they got up to, and it's too far out from the next one to ask about upcoming plans. If you're wondering why introverts take their sick days on Wednesdays, there's your answer.

There isn't an obvious solution to this problem, although abolishing Wednesdays altogether, for the betterment of workplace mental health, is an option. We suggest getting in contact with your union.

Monday	Tuesday	Wednesday	Thursday	Friday
'Get up to anything interesting on the weekend?'		**FUCK!**	'Plans for the weekend?'	

EXPERT INSIGHT

'I once met a consultant who specialised in teaching people how to make small talk. The weather was lovely that day. It looked like it was going to be a bit overcast, but we were really lucky.'

James Schloeffel

Small talk in a lift

If you work in a building with a lift, you will be faced daily with the prospect of being stuck in a 3-square-metre metal capsule with a colleague you barely know making uncomfortable small talk while you anxiously look up at the numbers, which don't seem to be changing fast enough. This event will generally last about 7–8 seconds, although it will feel like 7–8 hours.

We should mention that this experience is different for Americans, who generally see being in close proximity to a virtual stranger as 'fun' or 'an opportunity to promote myself'. (It's not surprising that the term 'elevator pitch' was coined by Americans – they are used to walking into a new space and familiarising everyone with their name, job title, salary range and favourite leisure pursuits without being asked.)

If you work in an office with a lift, we recommend the following precautions.

Never take the lift
Taking the stairs multiple times a day is tricky if you work on the eightieth floor, but just imagine the prospect of being stuck in a confined space with the CEO and you'll be up the stairs in no time. Great for your step count too.

Pretend to be on your phone
This is a classic tactic that generally works. You don't even need to talk – a simple point to your earbuds and a smile is all it takes to let others know to leave you alone. Just make sure your phone is on silent so it doesn't ring while you're pretending to be on a call.

Initiate 'the nod'
Mature adults know that an exchange of a small nod, accompanied by slightly smiling pursed lips, is all that's required to signal that there will be no talking during this lift journey.

EXAMPLE CONVERSATION IN A LIFT

If you do find yourself in a lift where you need to make small talk, the rule is generally to use the word 'busy' as much as possible.

PERSON 1: Hi, how are you? You keeping busy?

PERSON 2: Yep, busy busy!

PERSON 1: Good to be busy!

PERSON 2 Definitely! Better to be busy than not busy! You busy?

PERSON 1: So busy!

PERSON 2: Good to be busy!

PERSON 1: Yes, it is good to be busy! Busy weekend planned?

PERSON 2 Pretty busy. But not as busy as last weekend. You?

PERSON 1: Very busy. I'm getting divorced because my husband fu ... *[conversation cut short due to person arriving at their floor]*

SMALL TALK DAMPENERS

If you find yourself stuck with a colleague waiting for a meeting to begin, here are some phrases to help prevent your colleague from wanting to engage you in small talk.

- 'My niece just had a baby. I've got lots of photos.'
- 'I find it so interesting that people don't like my Pokemon card collection.'
- 'Recently I've been on the hunt for a good home-remedy for yeast infections.'
- 'I've been watching lots of videos on YouTube about Hitler.'

Banter

As any decent set of company Values will tell you, you need to mix up all of the hard work with a bit of Fun from time to time. It all adds to the jovial 'dynamic' culture that was promised in the job ad.

Here are some hilarious workplace one-liners that never stop being funny, even after the two-hundredth telling.

Someone arrives at work dressed more formally than usual
YOU: 'Job interview, eh?'

Someone leaves 15 minutes early because they have an appointment
YOU: 'Half-day today?'

The new person arrives for their second day
YOU: 'You came back!'

Swings

Roundabouts

A totally meaningless phrase that makes no sense

EXPERT INSIGHT

'Some people find small talk annoying because it often leads to being exposed to meandering anecdotes from people you hardly know about their personal lives. Which actually reminds me of something that happened to me last weekend when I tried to go fly-fishing with my stepson's brother-in-law and his mates, and we arrived but nobody had booked a spot at the cafe that we always try to go to before we head out and then luckily some people left so we were able to get a spot anyway. Sorry, what were we talking about?'

Charles Firth

UNIT 3: SECURING A NEW JOB

ONCE EVERY FEW YEARS YOU WILL GET SICK OF THE BULLSHIT AT YOUR CURRENT COMPANY AND KID YOURSELF INTO THINKING THAT THERE WILL BE LESS BULLSHIT ELSEWHERE. THIS IS KNOWN AS 'THE GRASS IS ALWAYS LESS FERTILISED WITH BULLSHIT ON THE OTHER SIDE' PHENOMENON.

FOLLOW OUR TIPS FOR SECURING YOUR DREAM ROLE.

How to decode job ads

Job advertisements have their very own language. They won't say something straightforward like 'We need a new junior receptionist'. Instead, they will say 'We are seeking a motivated, passionate self-starter with 25 years' experience to join our dynamic, fast-paced team. $30–35k p.a.'

To be successful, you will need to know how to decode these ads. Here are some common phrases with their translations.

PHRASE: 'Self-starter'
EXAMPLE: 'This is a great opportunity for a motivated self-starter looking to thrive.'
MEANING: 'We have absolutely no management systems in place.'

PHRASE: 'Diversity'
EXAMPLE: 'Our commitment to diversity means fifty per cent of our staff are women.'
MEANING: 'Sixty per cent of our junior and mid-level staff are women. Ninety percent of our senior staff are men.'

PHRASE: 'Dynamic'
EXAMPLE: 'Join our dynamic, fast-paced team.'
MEANING: 'We're not really sure what this means, but we needed another adjective.'

PHRASE: 'Bring your whole self to work'
EXAMPLE: 'We value diversity and encourage people to bring their whole self to work.'
MEANING: 'You can totally be yourself, as long as it aligns with our Values and Behaviours document, which we will interpret in any way we want if we don't like you.'

PHRASE: 'Inclusive'
EXAMPLE: 'We're proud of our inclusive culture.'
MEANING: 'For one week a year our logo changes to a rainbow.'

PHRASE: 'Attention to detail'
EXAMPLE: 'Attention to detail is essential in ths roal.'
MEANING: 'We have no attention to detail.'

PHRASE: 'Fast-paced'
EXAMPLE: 'Join our dynamic, fast-paced team.'
MEANING: 'For legal reasons we cannot explicitly discriminate on age, but definitely do not apply if you're over twenty-five.'

PHRASE: 'Team player'
EXAMPLE: 'We're looking for a team player who is ready to make an impact.'
MEANING: 'Please do not bring any opinions or ideas of your own.'

PHRASE: 'Passionate'
EXAMPLE: 'We're looking for a passionate self-starter to join our growing business.'
MEANING: 'We expect you to work weekends.'

PHRASE: 'Values-led organisation'
EXAMPLE: 'We're a values-led organisation that puts our purpose at the heart of everything we do.'
MEANING: 'We did an off-site brainstorm session with an external consultant last year where we wrote down the words 'honesty', 'inclusion', 'integrity' and another word I can't remember right now on a whiteboard and then pinned a print-out up in the staff kitchen.'

PHRASE: 'Vibrant'
EXAMPLE 1: 'We have a vibrant office culture.'
MEANING: 'We have a ping-pong table.'
EXAMPLE 2: 'We have a vibrant office culture and a growing team.'
MEANING: 'We have a ping-pong table, but it is now used as a desk.'

PHRASE: 'Works well under pressure'
EXAMPLE: 'We're looking for a self-starter who works well under pressure.'
MEANING: 'We're understaffed, erratic and indecisive and we have absolutely no management systems in place.'

PHRASE: 'Salary = $70–90k'
MEANING: 'Salary = $70k'

Three tips for writing a great cover letter

Found a job to apply for? You'll need to write a cover letter. Be sure to follow these three rules.

Tip 1: Highlight your passion
While there are many different ways to write a cover letter, what's most important is that your central passion in life – the thing that gets you out of bed in the morning – coincidentally lines up precisely with the specific requirements listed in the job description. For example:
- 'I have a passion for leveraging data to optimise Stakeholder deliverables.'
- 'Delivering on key objectives for a mid-sized supplier in the pet food sector has always been a key aspiration of mine.'
- 'As a child, my dream was always to foster collaboration to achieve value-added outcomes.'
- 'For as long as I can remember, I have wanted to spearhead strategic initiatives in line with agreed business goals.'
- 'One of the things I love most is supporting the SRT to implement key change programs and ensuring they align with relevant data deliverables.'
- 'My hobbies include hiking, skiing and using governance frameworks to deliver key milestones in a fast-paced, dynamic environment.'

Tip 2: Say '_____ is in my DNA'

People used to talk about hair colour or blood type when referring to their DNA. These days it's more likely to be 'the telecommunications industry' or 'a passion for customer service'. Genetic scientists are still baffled at how the chromosomal makeup of a human in the twenty-first century has evolved in such a way.

Nevertheless, by referring to your DNA, you give the impression that you are, quite literally, made for the job, as if you came out of the womb with green eyes, brown hair and a passion for aligning outputs with Stakeholder wants and needs.

As with other more traditional genetic characteristics, your DNA traits should be fixed and unchangeable, right up until you apply for the next job.

Tip 3: Use this cover-letter checklist

Think carefully about the unique skills and personality traits you can bring to a role. Then use each one of these words instead:

- above-and-beyond
- big-picture focused
- detail-focused
- can-do
- motivated
- passionate
- people person
- problem-solver
- self-starter
- willing to learn
- works well unsupervised
- works well with others.

> **WANKERNOMICS TIP:**
> In a job interview, make sure to say you are outcomes-focused. Never admit you are actually income-focused.

What is onboarding?

The concept of onboarding was created in the early 2000s when someone in a People & Culture department got so bored they took a tab of acid, started hallucinating and mistakenly thought they were welcoming a new staff member to an exotic Caribbean cruise, rather than their first day at an insurance company.

The word stuck and now companies around the world use onboarding to describe the process of familiarising people with anything from a new phone plan to a new safety procedure for cutting cakes at office birthday celebrations. But mostly, it's for starting new jobs.

What used to be summarised in the sentence, 'There's your desk, toilets are down the hall, your computer will be here in six-to-eight weeks', has now mutated into an elaborate three-month onboarding exercise involving endless forms, online modules and questionnaires, all of which you'll need to complete without a computer, because it's six-to-eight weeks away.

WANKERNOMICS TIP:
At least once a week, call someone with no real purpose and say 'Just touching base', even though you have no idea what that really means.

EXPERT INSIGHT

'One of the things I've learnt over many years as a People & Culture Director is how to use the words "many strong candidates", "cultural fit" and "at this time" to give people the impression I've read their cover letter, when in reality I pressed delete as soon as I realised I couldn't pronounce their surname.'

Penny Mason
People & Culture Director

Getting promoted

If getting a whole new job seems too much effort, there is another way to increase your pay packet: getting promoted.

A promotion is a great way to demonstrate to your co-workers that you're better than them, which studies show is the key motivation for most people to go to work in the first place.

Below, we've outlined three techniques for getting promoted. If you follow this advice, you are almost guaranteed to get promoted. Or sacked. Or possibly promoted, then sacked.

Step 1: Be terrible at your job

Being terrible at your job is not as much of an impediment to getting promoted as you might think. If you're the right level of terrible, it may give your boss the motivation to promote you, just to get you out of there.

Conversely, being good at your job can be a huge impediment to getting promoted. Confused? Consider it from the perspective of those managing you.

Imagine you are a competent employee who has enough experience to take on the next level of responsibility. You've updated your CV, regularly placed needlessly positive posts on LinkedIn, undergone extra training to keep up with the fast pace of technological innovation in your industry, and generally acquitted yourself with professionalism and dedication. As a result, you complete your work to an exceptional standard and deliver it on time, every time, without fuss or complaint.

Now imagine this from your boss's point of view. If they promote you, they'll be left with the hassle of having to train someone else to do your job. Plus, the promotion might see you leave the department entirely, meaning they can no longer skate along off the back of your above-average work ethic.

Step 2: Make a catastrophically expensive error

This is one of the easiest (and most fun) ways to score a promotion. The key is to make a mistake so egregious that your manager is also implicated by association.

Say your job is to run the payroll for 5000 employees. If you accidentally overpay ten workers, your boss can easily label you as an idiot and fire you. If anyone ever asks about it, your boss can just explain that it was a problem caused by a rogue employee (you).

However, if you overpay all 5000 workers, you've now created a problem so large that people will ask, 'Who was the idiot managing this person?' Once that happens, something magical occurs. It is now in your manager's interests to help you cover up the error and place the blame on systemic problems in your organisation, such as inadequate training, a lack of accountability safeguards by the board, or a lax approach to risk management.

Once the error has been dealt with, all anyone will ever remember is that you were the poor, innocent victim of your organisation's flawed systems, and your ascent through the organisation is assured. What's more, your boss will be happy to write a glowing recommendation just to get you out of there.

Step 3: Be related to senior management

This technique was invented by Julius Caesar in 44 BCE. Caesar wrote in his last will and testament that he wanted his great nephew Augustus to take over his position in the organisation he was running at the time (the Roman Empire). Unfortunately, because nepotism was so new, this approach was frowned upon, and Augustus had to murder quite a few senior managers before he was able to achieve his promotion in 27 BCE.

Luckily, nepotism is much more commonly accepted these days, which makes murdering less necessary in the promotion process.

Keep in mind that exploiting a relationship with senior management as a pathway to promotion is not for everyone, and fair enough too. We've heard horror stories of some people trying to use this method and then having to wait for up to 70 years for their promotion (see King Charles).

According to a 50-year study by Harvard University, the most effective way to become a CEO is to work hard, be open to new ideas and be the son of the CEO.

DON'T SAY:

'I've been sacked.'

DO SAY:

'I'm ready to embark on my next adventure.'

THE 'HOW MEANINGLESS IS YOUR JOB?' QUIZ

For every question that you answer 'yes' to, award yourself one point.

- [ ] Have you ever delayed sending an email until late at night to give the impression you are working hard?
- [ ] Have you ever spent at least twenty-five per cent of a meeting setting up the next meeting?
- [ ] Does your job title have the words 'special projects' or 'strategist' in it?
- [ ] Have you said the phrase 'I'm in back-to-back meetings all day' within the past month?
- [ ] Do you work in HR?
- [ ] Have you ever used Post-it notes or whiteboard markers as part of your job?
- [ ] If you failed to complete a project would the chance of someone dying as a result equal zero?
- [ ] Are you a futures trader?
- [ ] Does your office have a foosball table?
- [ ] If you answered every unread email in your inbox right now would the Middle East crisis remain unresolved?
- [ ] Is it impossible to explain what you do at work to a 5-year-old?

- ☐ Do you have anything even remotely to do with cryptocurrency?
- ☐ Have you used the term 'circle back' within the past week?
- ☐ Has the company you work for ever used the word 're-imagining' in their advertising?
- ☐ Have you ever used the phrase 'put some time back in your diary?'
- ☐ Do people on LinkedIn think your job is impressive?

0 POINTS: Don't lie – you're only cheating yourself. Please start again.

1-5 POINTS: You are essential to society and probably excruciatingly smug about it.

6-10 POINTS: Your job is meaningless.

11+ POINTS: You are a consultant.

UNIT 4: COLLABORATION

IN TODAY'S WORKING WORLD, COLLABORATION IS A MUST. THERE IS SIMPLY NOTHING THAT CANNOT BE IMPROVED BY TAKING ON BOARD THE SPONTANEOUS, RANDOM, UN-THOUGHT-THROUGH IDEAS OF UNQUALIFIED PEOPLE LOOKING TO IMPRESS EACH OTHER.

As any collaboration evangelist will tell you, two heads are always better than one, but thirty to forty heads are even better still. Adding in a few more heads on top of that probably doesn't hurt either, particularly if it means taking on board the thoughts of an arbitrary Key Stakeholder, or the CEO's friend from high school.

Offices across the world have been completely redesigned in order to more easily facilitate two or more people working together on a task that was previously done quite sufficiently by one. Core Values in businesses large and small have been updated to include the word 'collaborative' to reflect the importance of doing everything together.

We're all for the collaboration revolution. After all, there's nothing better than presenting something you've been working on within your area of expertise, say JavaScript coding, and then getting a 'build' from Kylie in Marketing who reckons it would look better in orange.

It's a bit like a pilot being forced to take on feedback from Terry in row 26 about the correct technique for landing a 787. But unfortunately, unlike a pilot, you don't have a locked door between you and everyone else, so you're going to have to learn to play along.

Phrases you should use to sound collaborative
- 'Let's loop in Terry.'
- 'Let's jump on a Zoom real quick to ideate further.'
- 'Shall we jump in a meeting room to blue-sky it?'
- 'Meagan, do you have any builds on the digital piece?'
- 'Let's set up a co-creation session with Vince's team before we circle back to Jennifer.'

For further tips on Collaboration, check out the Workshops, brainstorming and ideation section in Unit 5: Meetings (page 140).

IF THE WHEEL WAS INVENTED TODAY

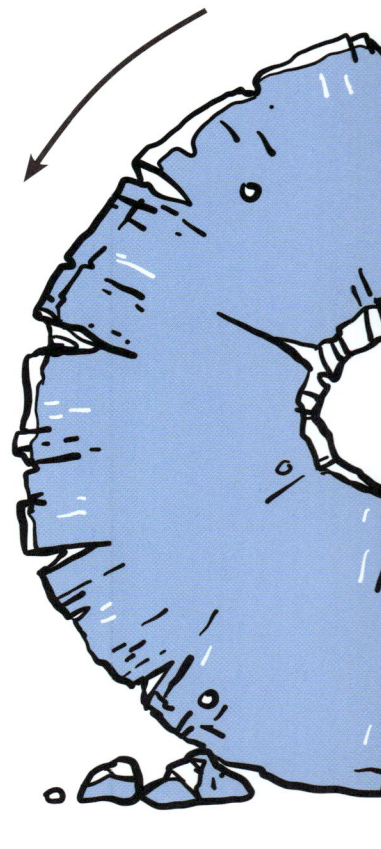

INTERN: 'Hey guys, I just invented the wheel!'

PRODUCT MANAGER: 'Wow. Great start, Mia! Let's get in a room and ideate it further!'

MARKETING MANAGER: 'I like it. But circles are very last year. Can we try a triangle-shaped wheel instead, maybe?'

LEGAL: 'I can see why you like it, but we're opening ourselves up to litigation by having something that moves. Can you humour me by putting together a version that doesn't move?'

FINANCE: 'Do we really need the whole wheel? I'm thinking we make it a semi-circle and halve costs.'

TECH: 'Can we add wi-fi for no reason at all?'

FACILITATOR: 'Some really great builds there, everyone. So I think after taking on board everyone's input, it's clear that we should make it into a star shape.'

PEOPLE & CULTURE: 'It's very circle-centric. We need to be welcoming to all shapes and sizes.'

CEO: 'My wife likes stars. Let's make it a star shape.'

MIDDLE MANAGER (WHO IS ALSO A DAD): 'Let's not re-invent the wheel here, guys!!!!'

UNION REP: 'My concern is that this wheel will put the jobs of hundreds of thousands of slaves in danger.'

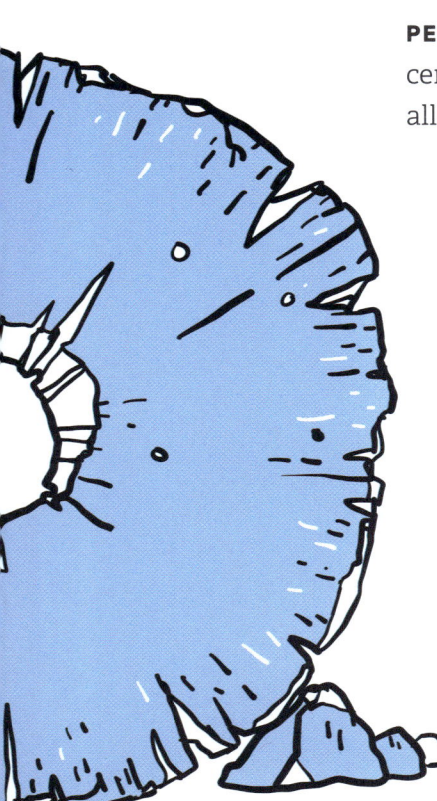

BRAND: 'Before we rush into inventing the wheel, I think we should take a step back and ask ourselves, what are the brand values of the wheel?'

DON'T SAY:

'I chatted to someone else in another department.'

DO SAY:

'I am breaking down the silos'

as if you're a farmer who has inexplicably decided to deconstruct a row of 200-cubic-metre grain storage facilities in order to foster better working practices.

Group editing

Group editing tools like Microsoft Word Track Changes are great for taking a piece of writing and making it worse, bit by bit.

The concept is straightforward: one person puts their heart, soul and expertise into creating a document, which their colleagues then thoroughly ruin with a series of competing, hastily added, incomprehensible changes.

If you have the opportunity to provide feedback on another colleague's work, and you feel so bored you want to do something disruptive, there are a number of different comment styles you can use to throw everything into disarray.

The contradictory comment
A great way to amuse yourself is to add a comment that totally refutes someone else's. So if Richard from Consumer Affairs has written 'Too long, please cut back', add a comment that says 'Feels a bit abrupt. Can we flesh this out a little?' It'll confuse the hell out of whoever has to edit the document and also pretty quickly establish who pulls the most weight out of you and Richard.

The open-ended comment
Having the appearance of being significant, while providing no meaningful direction whatsoever, this style of comment can single-handedly create hours of extra work.
- 'Can we say this?'
- 'Not sure about this.'
- 'Is Terry Donaldson across this?'

The hand grenade

Sometimes it's fun to create more work for someone for no real reason at all. Here are some example comments to consider:

- 'Let's set up a separate meeting to discuss this section.'
- 'Can you add in a para that talks to the work Brad Farley did on this last year? I've attached a 3000-word document for you to read and then summarise into two sentences.'

The let's-check-with-Legal comment

'Need to check this with Legal' is a catch-all comment that you can attach to pretty much any phrase in a document in order to create more work for the document's creator.

While the phrase in question will usually be legally valid, now that you've added the comment 'Need to check with Legal', it will need to be checked by Legal. Fun!

WHAT IS CO-CREATION?

Co-creation is a special type of collaboration involving Stakeholders, in which people with no relevant expertise are not only asked for their input on something, but actively encouraged to contribute to its design, thus ensuring that the final product is a horrific compromise of terrible ideas and superfluous opinions.

Co-creation, at least to date, has tended to be confined to logo designs, TV commercials, mission statements and other marketing-led creations. But it's only a matter of time before a client is asked to help co-create the engineering calculations for a new bridge or the active ingredients in a vaccine in the name of Stakeholder buy-in.

The passive-aggressive comment

Passive aggression is a core skill in any workplace and the comments section on a document is a great place to sharpen your skills.

- 'Not the words I would have chosen, but OK.'
- 'What you've written here seems entirely wrong, but maybe I've just misunderstood?'
- 'A good first attempt at this.'
- 'If you're comfortable saying that, then OK.'

The aggressive-aggressive comment

- 'Not the words I would have chosen. Are you a fucking idiot?'

Straight-up violent

- '????'
- 'No.'

The cheerful-but-deadly comment

Cajole your prey with an upbeat tone in the first half of your comment and then utterly crush their spirit in the second half.

- 'LOVE what you've done here! Can we cut it back by eighty per cent pls?'
- 'This is bang on. Can you humour me by starting again and writing an entirely different version?'

The Purpose/Vision/Mission/Values comment

There's no better way to derail a perfectly structured document than to demand that it tie in with some arbitrary corporate Mission Statement or set of Values that was created at a management away-day earlier in the year.

- 'Can we link this sentence about the structural engineering requirements of elevator shafts to our Values of "Respect, honesty and collaboration" please?'
- 'This section on upcoming wage reductions needs to ladder up to our Purpose Statement of "Putting our people at the centre of everything we do". Please adjust.'

ASK WANKERNOMICS

Q: How ~~the fuck~~ do I turn off Track Changes once I've turned it on?

A: You can't.

UNIT 5:
MEETINGS

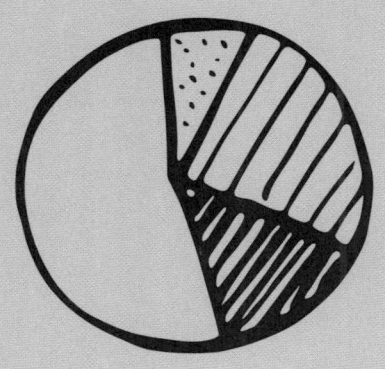

RESEARCH SHOWS THAT IF YOU WORK IN AN OFFICE JOB, YOU WILL SPEND AN AVERAGE OF 22 YEARS OF YOUR LIFE IN MEETINGS.*

Meetings are so abundant that, statistically speaking, it is almost certain you have either just finished a meeting, you are on your way to one, or you are in one right now, reading this book with your video turned off while someone in the background asks if we should 'do a quick around the grounds'.

It goes without saying that meetings are totally useless. Nothing valuable or innovative or interesting has ever resulted from a meeting. Isaac Newton did not, as it turns out, invent calculus at a 9.30 am stand-up. Marie Curie did not discover radium during a weekly status update.

Yet meetings are utterly inescapable. If we didn't have meetings, we'd all get our day's work done by around 9.30 am each morning, we'd be home by 10 am and the entire corporate capitalist system would collapse.

No matter what stage of your career you are in, you're never far away from someone saying, 'Let's put some time in the diary' or 'Should we put aside an hour each week to sit around a table and repeat what we said the week before?'

Despite meetings being utterly useless, having a lot of them is important because it sounds awfully cool to say you're in

* Per year

back-to-back meetings all day. Nothing is more embarrassing, or career limiting, than saying you have a clear afternoon in which you plan to get some work done. So for goodness sake, make sure your calendar is always full.

There are four main types of meetings:
- recurring meetings (status updates, check-ins, WIPs, weekly stand-ups, etc.)
- all-hands meetings
- one-off meetings
- workshops, brainstorming and ideation.

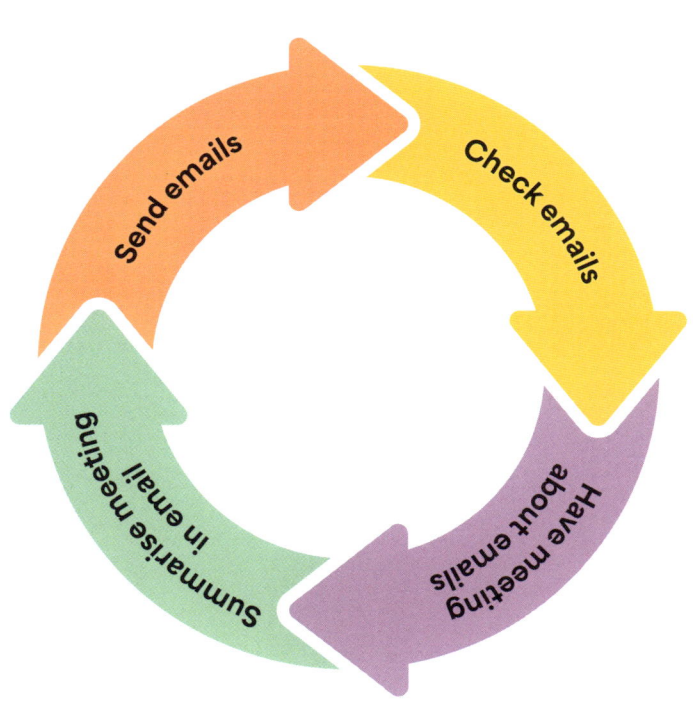

Recurring meetings

In these meetings, a group of employees take turns providing an excruciating update about what they've been working on over the past 7 days, while everyone else pretends to listen. Each update will be virtually identical to the one given last week and relevant to no-one in the meeting except the person talking.

These meetings are scheduled, usually by managers, to give the impression that something productive is taking place. Often, they will begin by running through the minutes or actions from the previous meeting, an agonising process that usually takes around 3-4 hours. At the end of the meeting, the updated minutes are sent around for everyone to ignore.

It is essential that, even once the initial purpose of a recurring meeting has long since passed, it continues forever without being cancelled. That way, you can accumulate more and more meetings until your entire week is nothing more than a series of status updates, WIPs and catch-ups about projects that finished years ago and that you wouldn't have time to work on anyway because you have too many meetings.

DID YOU KNOW?

A British organisation still has in place a weekly 'ink well supplies WIP' that was first set up in 1947. Despite the organisation no longer using ink wells, no-one is able to cancel the meeting (the meeting organiser died in 1968), so it continues to this day, at 11 am each Wednesday.

How to survive a recurring meeting

Regardless of how little your work has progressed since the last meeting, it is essential that you give a sense of movement and activity. Your boss didn't get to where she is today by saying, 'No updates from me.'

✗ **DON'T SAY:** 'I've done literally zero work on that project since last week.'
✓ **DO SAY:** 'That's a work in progress.'

✗ **DON'T SAY:** 'Shit, I forgot to speak to Finance about that.'
✓ **DO SAY:** 'The conversations with Finance are ongoing.'

✗ **DON'T SAY:** 'I am nowhere near finishing writing that document.'
✓ **DO SAY:** 'It's a living, breathing document.'

Using unverifiable statistics matched with random acronyms can also be a successful tactic.

💬 **MEETING ORGANISER:** What's the update on the progress of Project Alpha, Sue?

💬 **SUE:** The BBP is making progress on integrating the CNI into the M2M. We've seen a twenty-six per cent integration rate already and should have a full AWN by 10 March.

💬 **MEETING ORGANISER:** Sounds like there's a lot of great stuff happening there, thanks Sue.

HOW MEETINGS REPRODUCE

Research has shown that the number of meetings in an organisation expands in much the same way as rabbits in a rabbit colony.

'We should probably set up another session on this.'

'Shall we establish a subcommittee to deal with this?'

'How are you placed next Thursday to continue this conversation?'

'Let's set up a regular weekly check-in to make sure things are on track.'

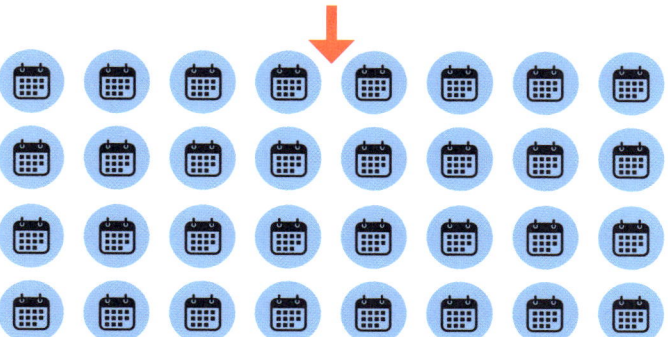

'How about we put some time in the diary every second Monday for a quick status update?'

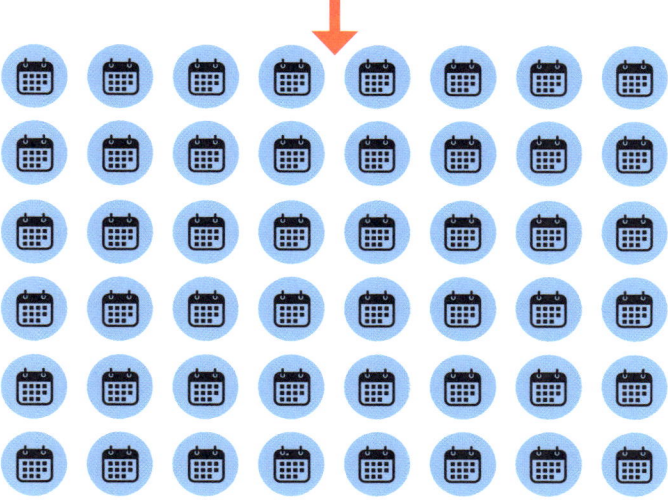

Even though it had some success in reducing the number of rabbits in Australia, unfortunately, it is against most HR company policies to intentionally introduce the myxoma virus into the workplace.

All-hands meetings (also called 'town hall' meetings)

An all-hands meeting is a chance to get everyone in the organisation together to use words like 'same page', 'aligned' and 'singing from the same song sheet'.

An all-hands meeting could almost always have just been an email, but instead tends to be a 90-minute endurance test of your willingness to live.

The exception is when an all-hands meeting is placed in your diary 30 minutes before the meeting starts, in which case you are almost certainly all getting fired.

As there are usually limited opportunities to interact in these meetings, our only advice is to join remotely, turn off your camera and find a good book.

DEFINITION

'Meeting' [noun]

A group of people who have no idea what the meeting is about, all trying to give the impression that they do, while simultaneously trying to avoid being lumped with any additional work, while also trying to look smart.

WANKERNOMICS TRANSLATOR

PHRASE:

'Can we get a BDA update on the SST please, John?'

↓

MEANING:

'No idea, but it sounds fucking cool.'

One-off meetings

There are times when a meeting will be called for a specific reason. In almost all cases, no-one – including the person who called the meeting – will be able to define what that specific reason actually is.

The trick to these meetings is to get through the allotted time without letting on that you don't know what the meeting is about, while simultaneously trying to avoid picking up any additional work, while also trying to appear smart.

Pulling this off takes skill. Here are some best-practice phrases you can use in your next meeting to avoid ever having to let on that you don't know what is going on.

- 'Let's pick that up at a local level.'
- 'Shall we take that offline?'
- 'Before jumping into the details, let's take a step back.'
- 'Do you want to have a run at that, George?'
- 'What's the key ask here?'
- 'That's more of a Terry Donaldson question.'
- 'We probably should hold off on that until Terry's in the room.'
- 'Let's put a pin in that and circle back later.'
- 'Before we begin, can we talk about the mess in the kitchen?'
- 'We should probably set up a separate session on that.'

While these phrases will help, unfortunately everyone else will be doing the same thing: all trying not to let on that they don't know what the meeting is about, while trying to avoid taking on any additional work, while also trying to appear smart. As a result, this is what invariably unfolds:

PAUL: We should probably get started. Do you want to kick us off, Fiona?

FIONA: Happy for you to do that.

PAUL: OK, sure. Let's first quickly go around the room and get everyone to introduce themselves, given Priya's just started this week and doesn't necessarily know everyone.

[… 40 minutes later]

PAUL: Thanks for that, everyone. Fiona, do you want to start by running us through the relevant issues here?

FIONA: Let's take that offline and circle back later. I was thinking maybe Rick could start us off by taking us through his top-line thoughts on what we want to get out of this meeting.

RICK: Great idea. But before I do that, I think we first need to ask ourselves, 'What is the key ask here?' Tony, you'd have some thoughts on that?

TONY: Definitely. But are we putting the cart before the horse?

RICK: How do you mean?

TONY: By jumping into the granular detail before taking a step back and defining our Why.

FIONA: He's right. What is our Why?

PAUL: And does it ladder up to our overarching Purpose Statement?

💬 **TONY:** Exactly.

💬 **PAUL:** We should probably set up a separate session on this.

💬 **RICK:** Is Sally Walsh across this?

💬 **PAUL:** No, I hadn't thought of that. We need to make sure Sally is aligned before we go any further or we could have an alignment issue. Priya, do you want to set up a dialogue with Sally to make sure she's aligned?

💬 **PRIYA:** Well, you can't set up a dialogue without breaking down the silos. Do you want to break down the silos, Rick?

💬 **RICK:** Sure, but you can't break down the silos until you've got Stakeholder buy-in.

💬 **PRIYA:** Do we have Stakeholder buy-in?

💬 **RICK:** That's more of a Terry Donaldson question.

💬 **TONY:** Is Terry here?

💬 **RICK:** No, he couldn't make it – got caught up in another meeting.

💬 **PAUL:** Well, there's not much point continuing with this meeting without Terry here. Should we wind this up for now and reconvene next week?

💬 **FIONA:** Sounds like the best thing to do. Priya, do you want to send around the meeting minutes?

💬 **PRIYA:** Happy for you to do that …

[This continues in a loop until the allotted meeting time is up.]

DON'T SAY:

'I have to leave this meeting at the scheduled time like everyone else.'

DO SAY:

'I have a hard-stop at twelve.'

Workshops, brainstorming and ideation

The concept of brainstorming started in the 1950s when some tediously upbeat American decided it would be a good idea to place a bunch of random people in a soulless boardroom with some butcher's paper and a bowl of Mentos and ask them to think outside the box.

Since then, brainstorming has infiltrated every part of modern organisations, to the point where you can't decide where to go for a team lunch these days without a flip chart and a dozen colourful markers.

At some point in the 2010s, a group of creative change agents and thought-leadership evangelists decided that the term 'brainstorm' was not irritating enough and so they changed it to 'ideation'.*

Realising they could charge at least 200 per cent more for an ideation session than a brainstorm session, consultants and advertising agencies latched on to the new term, which means we're probably stuck with it forever, or at least until someone comes up with something worse, like 'creationationing' or 'knowledge solutioning'.

---

* While at first glance 'ideation' sounds like a smart new technology for powering combustion engines, it actually just means 'thinking'.

THE PURPOSE OF WORKSHOPS

Creative agencies and middle managers love workshops because they give the impression that something imaginative – even magical – is being created, when what is actually being created is a bunch of half-baked, un-thought-through ideas that will be forgotten as soon as the session is over.

Brainstorming is also popular because it is non-hierarchical. Everyone – from the junior intern to the most experienced subject matter expert – gets to put their ideas forward, before the most senior person in the room's idea is finally agreed upon.

DID YOU KNOW?

Forty-six per cent of the trees cleared in the Amazon rainforest are used to make flip charts for break-out sessions in workshops.

HOW TO LOOK LIKE A GENIUS IN WORKSHOPS

Workshops and brainstorming sessions are used for everything from new product development to choosing a theme for the office Christmas party, so it's unlikely you'll be able to avoid them.

Often lasting for hours at a time, they are incredibly boring, but also an invaluable opportunity to increase your status within an organisation. In most workplaces, being able to talk bullshit is highly regarded, and a blue-sky ideation workshop is a great place to do it. If played correctly, you can look like a genius *and* zone out for most of the workshop, giving you time to plan your next holiday in your head.

The trick is to appear engaged by occasionally dropping in meaningless-but-important-sounding questions or statements that give the impression you are deeply engrossed in a topic in which you have invaluable expertise. Here are some examples to try in your next brainstorm session.

> **DID YOU KNOW?**
> If you placed all of the meetings happening in the world right now end-to-end, you would be considered incredibly weird.

'Are we in danger of reinventing the wheel here?'
While a corporate workshop has never been in danger of doing something as meaningful as transforming human transportation, by saying this phrase you'll plant a seed of doubt in your colleagues' minds about the usefulness of their ideas. Back to the drawing board for them and back to holiday planning for you.

'I just want to jump in here and echo Laura's last statement ...'
This is a proven strategy for standing out in any meeting. First, identify the most influential person in the meeting. Next, say that you want to echo what they've just said. Third, echo what they've just said. You magically gain all of the kudos without doing any of the work.

If echoing is not your thing, try piggybacking. You can say, 'Just to piggyback off what Laura was saying ...' and then repeat word-for-word what Laura was just saying.

Or say, 'If I understand this correctly ...' and then repeat whatever Laura just said.

DEFINITION

'Team-building exercise' [noun]

When a corporate training company hosts a well-established leisure activity like paintball or karate at 800 times the regular cost.

'What would Apple do?'

This applies to any workshop or meeting on any topic, regardless of whether it's related to Apple or not. How would Apple do iron-ore mining? Probably really badly because they're a phone company. But by saying this phrase, you'll sound switched-on and tech-savvy, and everyone will think you're an 'out-of-the-box' thinker.

More recently this phrase has occasionally been replaced with, 'What would Elon Musk do?' This could mean you are about to enter a discussion about anything from starting a colony on Mars to promoting a new cryptocurrency to helping finance a campaign for Donald Trump, so tread carefully.

'Let's remember that, at the end of the day, we are in the people business'

This is one of those phrases that sounds profound but is just an obvious statement of fact. No matter what industry you're in, your colleagues will sit up and take notice when you remind them that the company's customers are human.

'We need to put customers at the centre'

Nothing gets marketers and managers more excited than the idea of putting customers at the centre. You don't even need to say what they'll be at the centre of (although 'everything' will usually suffice). Just using the words 'customer' and 'centre' in the same sentence once per meeting will be enough for your colleagues to think you are the next Steve Jobs.

DON'T SAY:

'Let's sit in a soulless meeting room while we work our way through an agonising list of agenda items.'

DO SAY:

'Quick huddle?'

'We need to take a holistic approach'
Guaranteed to get heads nodding, this phrase can be used at any point in a brainstorm or ideation session. It gives the impression that you are considering a broader, bird's-eye perspective, when all you've done is put a few empty words together in a meaningless phrase.

'It's all about balance'
The reason brainstorming sessions rarely produce anything of value is that they tend to generate a series of disparate, often opposing, sometimes good ideas, which are then combined and watered down into a mediocre end output that everyone can agree on.

This is why the term 'it's all about balance' works so well. People are desperately trying to find a way to appease Ron, who thinks the new product launch should have a *Charlie's Angels* theme, and Kerrie, who thinks that's massively sexist. Sagely saying 'It's all about balance' provides the circuit breaker everyone is looking for and people will praise you for your level-headed, nuanced approach to business.

Other phrases to use in workshops
- 'Let's not presuppose what the focus groups might say on that.'
- 'Interesting build, Susan. What is the data saying on that?'
- 'Yes, but can we measure it?'

- 'Hmmm, good point, but does it ladder up to the overarching Purpose Statement?'
- 'Have we considered this from a Gen Z perspective?'
- 'Sarah, you'd have some thoughts on this, wouldn't you?'
- 'Have we considered the implications of AI?'
- 'Shall we whiteboard it?'
- 'Is Legal across this?'
- 'Do we need to set up another session on this?'
- 'Yes, but are we conflating two issues here?'
- 'Has this been signed off by SLT?'
- 'Stakeholder buy-in is key.'

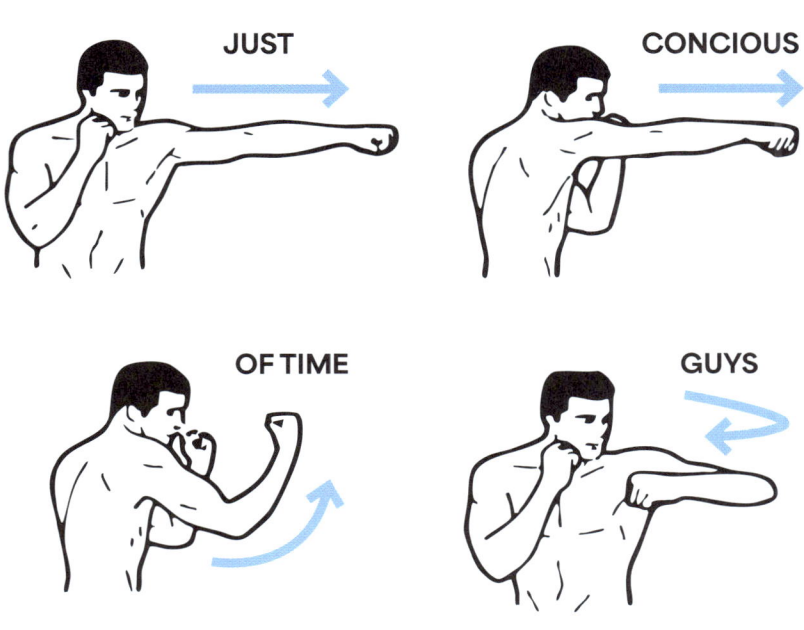

EXPERT INSIGHT

'We've always tried to give our child the opportunity to get ahead in life, which is why, since he was born, we only use workplace language when talking to him. The outcome has been astonishing. His first word was "optimisation". When he was hungry or tired, he quickly learnt to provide us with "360-degree feedback" rather than crying. And just the other day we overheard him telling his teddy bear that he was being "freed up to pursue future career opportunities" due to downsizing in his cubbyhouse operations. Fingers crossed, he might become a middle-manager one day.'

James Schloeffel

How to run a brainstorm session

Facilitating a brainstorm session or workshop can be intimidating. How are you going to fill 3 hours when all you've got is a blank slate, a blue sky and a dozen uninterested people? Here are some tips.

Always start by 'going around the room'
A great time-wasting tactic is to 'go around the room' and get attendees to introduce themselves (sometimes called 'going around the grounds' for online meetings).

Given that people always dramatically overestimate how interested other people are in hearing about their job, this will take at least 2 hours, and 8 if your workshop is being held in the United States.

Here's an example of a typical 'quick introduction' in a workshop.

- 'Hi, I'm Sally Walsh, heading up Customer Retention Management in Jim Weatherby's team, with a dotted line to Sarah Chong. My focus is around aligning best-practice functionalities with our SAP capabilities, with a view to … *[245,000 words removed for space reasons]* … 4-year-old cavoodle. And that's me!'

Always say 'no idea is a bad idea'

You should always start a brainstorm session with this phrase, even though everyone knows that there are loads of ideas that are astoundingly bad.

By kicking things off this way, you ensure you never have to use an ounce of judgement or show any conviction. You can simply make a long list of all the absurd shit people come up with and pass it off as 'facilitating creativity'.

If you do feel like breaking the mould a little, you can say 'Let's park that idea for now', which means 'Let's never speak of that idea ever again'.

Set up break-out groups

You can whittle away substantial chunks of time by splitting people into groups of six, giving them a flip chart and a vague topic, and asking them to present back to the group in 40 minutes.

People will become so focused on looking good in front of their peers that they won't even notice that the work they are doing has absolutely no purpose.

Seeing a bunch of adults stand up in front of their colleagues to explain some hastily developed ideas that 'the scribe' has scrawled onto some butcher's paper in coloured marker is a deeply peculiar feature of modern life, but you shouldn't think too hard about it, or you might start to question whether there's a point to your job at all.

Be sure to tell everyone to hand in their pieces of butcher's paper at the end of the session. It gives the impression that you'll compile the ideas into a central document, and not throw them straight in the bin.

Break-out groups work even better online, where you can split people into virtual rooms and then head to your couch for 40 minutes to watch an episode of your favourite show.

Run an icebreaker exercise

An icebreaker is a short game intended for kindergarten children but carried out by adults. It's designed as a fun way to relax a group into a session.*

Like the ships after which they are named, icebreakers are designed to shatter things – in this case, your will to live.

There is a three-step process for coming up with icebreaker ideas:

- **STEP 1:** Gatecrash a children's birthday party.
- **STEP 2:** Observe the games they play.
- **STEP 3**: Run the same games in a corporate workshop, but charge $550 an hour.

---

* Research has shown that icebreakers are neither fun nor relaxing. One recent study found that the phrase 'Let's kick off with a fun little icebreaker exercise' is the leading cause of heart attacks in the corporate sector.

THE WANKERNOMICS GOLDEN RULES OF MEETINGS

Number 1:
Ensure that meetings never finish early

You've allowed 60 minutes for the meeting, but you've got through everything in 34 minutes. Should you finish up and get on with something more productive? Of course not. You should pad out the final 26 minutes, repeating what has already been said, then reiterating the main points, then recapping them, then re-emphasising that those main points are really key moving forward until – shit, you've still got 6 minutes left – let's go through the next steps again and maybe go around the room to get everyone's final thoughts before finally, Paul says he has a hard stop and has to go so we can all leave now.

The only way to get around this rule is to say, 'We might be able to put some time back in your diary' (see page 159), in which case you will still waste 10 minutes recapping everything anyway, before finishing up 16 minutes early and then squandering it by having a 'sidebar' straight afterwards with someone who was in the same meeting, drilling down on the main points from the meeting you just had.

THE WANKERNOMICS GOLDEN RULES OF MEETINGS

Number 2: Always use the current meeting to set up the next meeting

You must spend at least twenty-five per cent of every meeting setting up the next meeting. That way you can ensure that your organisation is constantly trapped in a cycle of endless meetings and won't have enough time to reflect on the fact that the entire company could be run by two part-time workers and an AI robot.

TIME SPENT IN MEETINGS

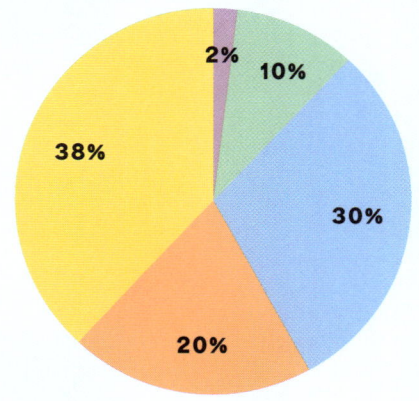

- Productive discussion
- Awkward small talk
- 'Let's quickly go around the room'
- 'Shall we go through the minutes from last week?'
- Setting up the next meeting

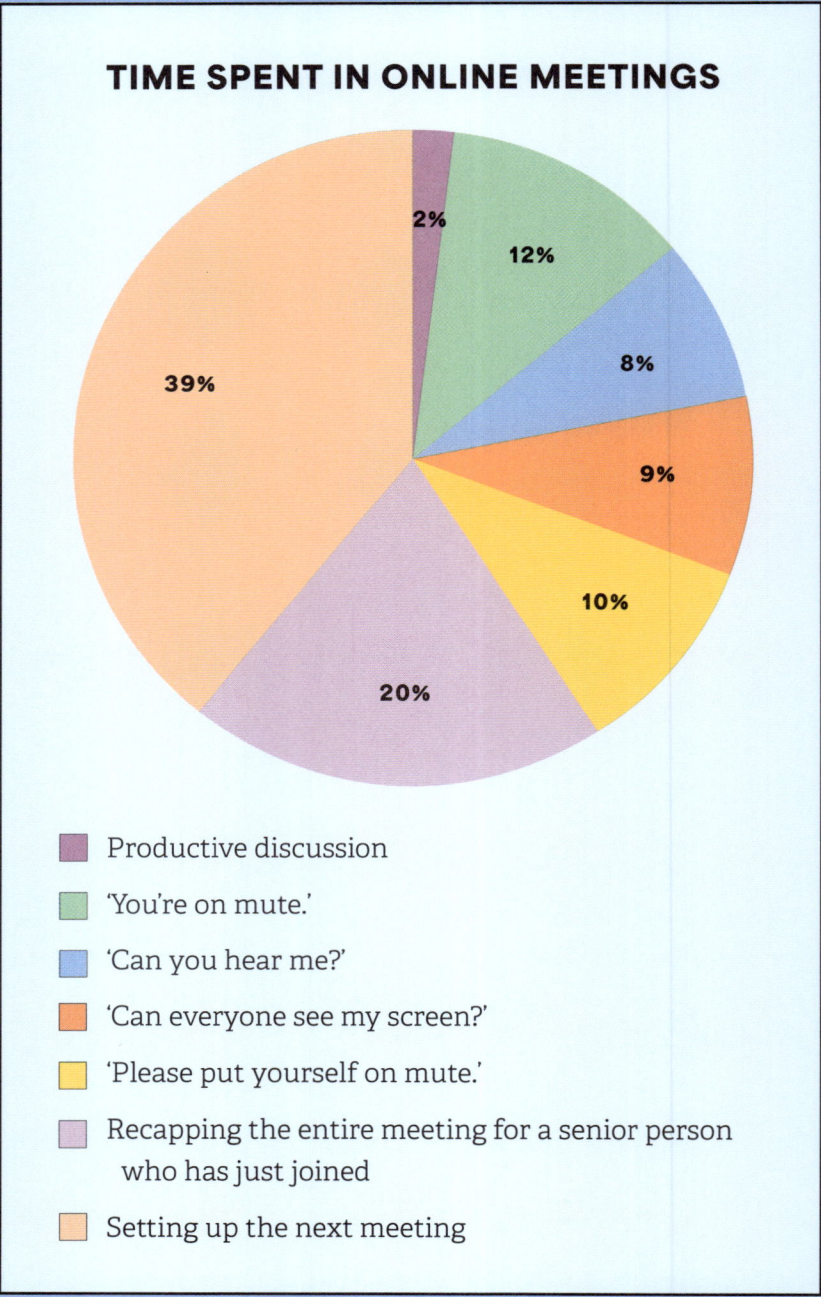

THINKING OUTSIDE THE BOX

It's a little-known fact, but prior to the late twentieth century, most creative thinking was done inside of boxes. People would routinely curl themselves up in a special box called a 'thinking box', sometimes for hours at a time, before emerging with an idea.

Einstein developed his theory of relativity while crouched in a cardboard box en route to the United States. Shakespeare wrote much of *Hamlet* squeezed into a thinking box he kept buried near the Thames.

The practice fell out of favour in the 1980s when a Creative Director at advertising agency Wieden+Kennedy ruptured a disc in his back while trying to develop a new slogan for Nike. Forced to think 'outside the box', he immediately came up with 'Just Do It', and never set foot inside his thinking box again.

Since then, thinking 'inside the box' has been very much frowned upon, not just by creative types, but by physiotherapists too. The phrase 'Let's make sure we think outside the box' is now used in offices around the world, with most people not realising its origins.

So, next time you sit in a small corporate meeting room with inadequate ventilation, thank your lucky stars that people aren't forced to think inside boxes anymore.

Meeting powerplays

Whether it's because you're shooting for a promotion, looking to impress a work colleague or just bored, there are times when you'll want to use a meeting as an opportunity to throw your weight around. There are a number of strategic manoeuvres you can employ to show everyone that you call the shots around here.

Say 'I have a hard stop'

While having a 'hard stop' simply means you have to leave the meeting at the scheduled, pre-agreed time like everyone else, announcing at the start of a meeting that 'I have a hard stop at 2.30 pm' immediately establishes you as someone who is not to be messed with. You have more important things to be doing and God help anyone who wastes your time. The meeting is now on your terms.

You can use the alternate phrase 'I have a hard end', but there's a risk it could be misinterpreted and you'll be forced to spend the afternoon re-reading the company's sexual harassment policy, so best to stick with hard stop.

✗ **DON'T SAY:** 'I have to leave this meeting at the scheduled time like everyone else.'
✓ **DO SAY:** 'I have a hard stop at twelve.'

Ask if there is an agenda

There's no better way to frazzle someone who's called a low-key meeting to discuss setting up a kitchen cleaning roster than to ask the whereabouts of the meeting's agenda. They'll nervously admit they haven't got one, you'll raise one eyebrow and let out a frustrated sigh, and you now run the meeting.

Say 'Are we missing a trick here?'
This phrase is best used towards the end of a meeting in which, to that point, you have remained silent.

It gives the impression that you have some stunning insight or solution that everyone else has overlooked without requiring you to actually say what that insight or solution is.

The phrase originated from the game bridge, which in

ACTIVITY

Try this fun activity to amuse yourself in your next meeting:
1. At some point in the meeting randomly say, 'I think we need to take a holistic approach here and consider all options.'
2. Watch everyone furiously nod in agreement.
3. Wait 5 minutes.
4. Say 'I think we need to take a more single-minded approach here and focus in on one core strategy.'
5. Watch everyone furiously nod in agreement.
6. Repeat.

many ways is similar to a corporate meeting – people play their cards close to their chest, try to outmanoeuvre their colleagues and are often lacking a heart.

Say 'Sorry, I've got to take this'

Nothing says 'I'm more important than you' than jumping onto a phone call mid-meeting. When you return to the meeting, say something like, 'Sorry, I just had to quickly sort out something above your paygrade'.

Say 'Yes, but does it align with our Purpose/Mission/Vision?'

Because no-one ever remembers what the company's Purpose or Mission or Vision Statement is, asking if someone's idea aligns with it (or ladders up to it) is the perfect way to undermine them. They'll say, 'Not sure.' You'll say, 'We might need to park that idea for now then,' and you'll get an immediate feeling of inflated self-importance.

Repeat what someone else has said, but in a louder voice

This strategy works particularly well for middle-aged men. It doesn't seem to work as well for women, for some reason. We did ask a woman once why this is, but we cut her off before she could finish explaining, so it remains a mystery.

Say you will 'Put some time back in the diary'

If you're running a meeting, a fun little phrase to say at the start is 'If we get through things quickly we might be able to put some time back in your diary'.

Of course, you could just say 'finish early'. But there's something really intoxicating about having the power to take someone's time and give it back, as if you're a parent giving out pocket money, or some sort of Time Lord, handing out little pieces of time that people then, bizarrely, *place in their diaries* – as if that is the way that time, or diaries, work.

> 'Oh look! I just opened up my diary and … sorry, what's that? Yeah, I know no-one has used a diary since 2004, but stay with me here. I opened up my diary and I found eight minutes that John Batterman gave me back during the FSA working-group meeting last week. I think I might use it to go out for lunch tomorrow. What a nice guy.'

DID YOU KNOW?

In ancient times, humans showed off their importance by wearing jewels or colourful clothing. These days they do it by saying 'I have back-to-back meetings all day'.

DON'T SAY:

'We finished early.'

DO SAY:

'We've put some time back in your diary'

as if you have no understanding of the working of diaries. Or time.

POWERPOINT PRESENTATIONS

Twelve compulsory steps for delivering a PowerPoint presentation

1. Never call it a PowerPoint presentation. Always call it either a deck or a pack (see Unit 1, Rule 29, page 65).
2. Say 'I'm just going to share my screen? Can everyone see my screen?'
3. Make sure you close the porn tabs. *[In hindsight, that should've been step 2.]*
4. Start off your presentation by saying 'We can race through this', as if it will only take 5 minutes to go through 422 slides.
5. Spend at least 40 minutes on the first slide.
6. Make sure each slide contains at least 5000 words of text. Reduce the font size to 4-point so it all fits but is unintelligible.
7. Immediately apologise for having too much on the slide.
8. Read out every single word on each slide.
9. Have one funny slide, which includes a meme you downloaded from Google Images.
10. Immediately regret putting in the funny slide.
11. When you finally get to the interesting content in your presentation, say 'We can probably just skip through this' and then race through the last 280 slides in 90 seconds.
12. Realise you've run out of time and say you'll have to set up another session.

MEETINGS (AS DESCRIBED BY DAVID ATTENBOROUGH)

'High up on the forty-third floor of a city office tower, we find one of nature's most intricate and curious rituals: the meeting.

'Here we see the senior male executive, eager to impress his colleagues, begin an elaborate performance. First, he apologises for being late, name-dropping another business-critical project he is working on for the CEO, before reminding those present he has a hard stop at 2 pm.

'Next, he asks if there is an agenda for this meeting, before restating his importance by stepping out briefly to take a call.

'Back in the room now, he begins the next stage of his impressive dance. Here we hear him mimicking the female, repeating the point she has just made, but in a louder, more forceful voice. It is only a matter of time before he – yes, here it is now – he has claimed the idea as his own. Fascinating.

'Then, in a final flurry of activity, he rises up from his chair for no reason at all, pensively walks around the room, and, pausing for dramatic effect, says, "Are we missing a trick here?"'

– David Attenborough, from his new BBC documentary *Wankers in Meetings*

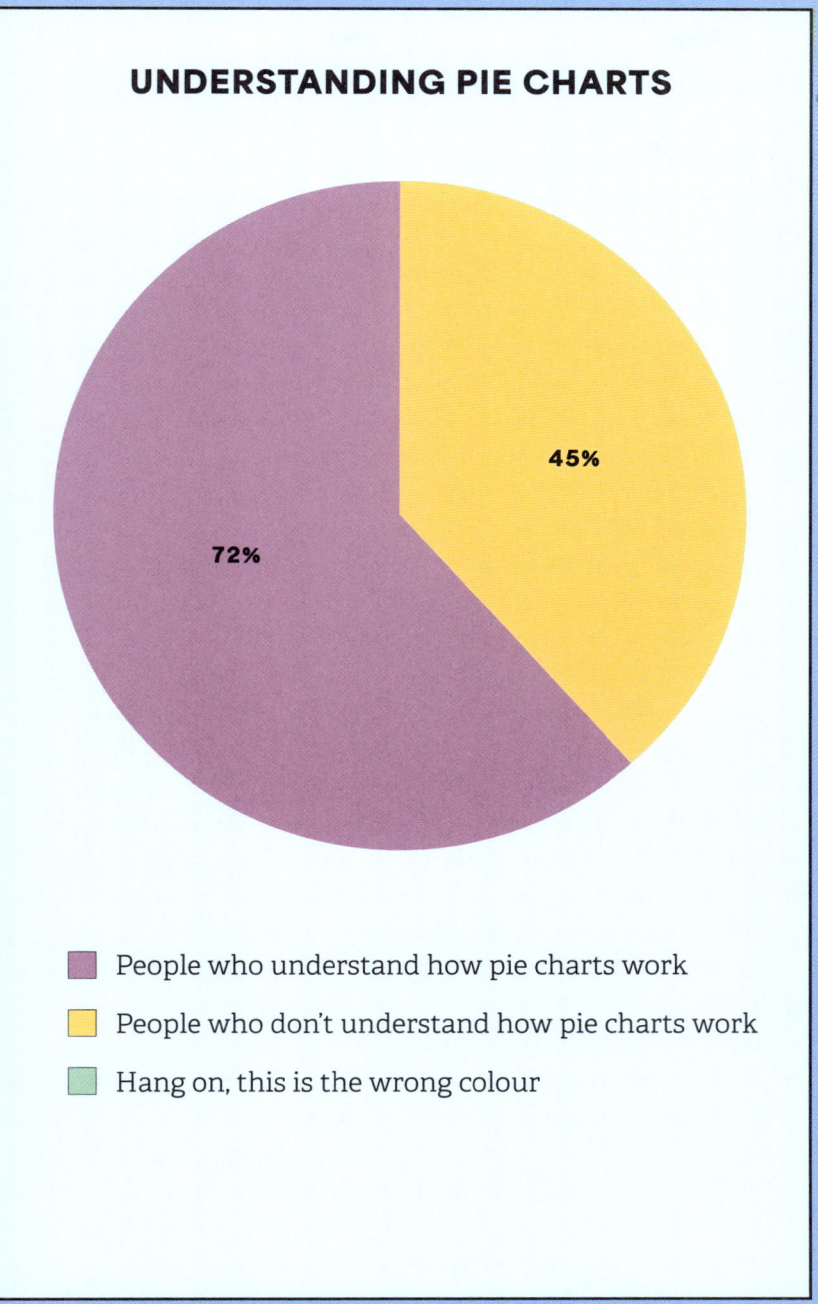

UNIT 6:
THE PURPOSE OF HR

[This page left intentionally blank]

[This page left intentionally blank]

UNIT 7: LINKEDIN

LAUNCHED IN 2002 AS A SIMPLE WAY TO UPLOAD YOUR RESUME ONLINE, LINKEDIN QUICKLY MORPHED INTO A PECULIAR FORM OF TORTURE WHEREBY PEOPLE SHARE UPDATES ABOUT THEIR WORK AND OTHER PEOPLE PRETEND TO CARE.

Unfortunately, you can only hold out for so long without a LinkedIn profile. Here's how to make it work for you.

RULE 1 OF LINKEDIN:

Be inexplicably excited about everything

Starting a new job? You're thrilled to announce it.

Working on a new project? You're delighted to be a part of it.

Received an email from a colleague this morning? You're super excited to start the journey of opening it up and seeing what it might entail.

The joy is inescapable. Whether you're announcing your latest career promotion, sharing the fact that your company has re-designed its website or commenting on an article about taxation law, you must project the level of enthusiasm you'd usually only muster while under the influence of MDMA.

Everywhere you look people are inspired, honoured, ecstatic, eager, delighted, energised, or just plain excited to have had the immense privilege to work on such an interesting, important project.

They enthusiastically share their company's new brand values with the misjudged assumption that anyone else would give even the tiniest shit.

They write things like, 'Exciting new changes coming for the insurance industry', without stopping to consider that the words 'exciting' and 'insurance industry' should never appear in the same sentence.

They add comments like 'Love this!' or 'So exciting!' on posts about new product launches from global detergent brands.

They announce that they've successfully completed an industry certification in environmentally responsible folder management. And what's worse, other people respond with comments like 'Congrats!' and 'Woohoo!', thus feeding the whole pointless-as-piss posting machine.

And if you think it's only influencers or life coaches who are so happy all the time on LinkedIn, think again. Scroll a few seconds on the platform and you'll realise your real-world friends - people you thought would never fall for this shit - have also gone insane.

That guy from university who was once a cynical, anti-corporate Arts student in a punk band is now 'Excited to be working on such an important and inspiring project in the Risk Assessment Team at Allianz.' That friend in your book club who was complaining about her boss last week? She's 'Thrilled to be spearheading a new engagement project in the digital space.'

Unfortunately, you can't opt out of LinkedIn - it's now a compulsory part of capitalist existence. And you certainly can't get by with banal-but-honest posts like 'Moderately unfussed about starting a new project this week.' People might think you are not utterly thrilled about your job. So your only choice is to join in wholeheartedly on the happy-speak.

How do you amass so much enthusiasm without taking class A drugs? Follow the examples below.

- ✗ **DON'T SAY:** 'I spent this morning re-formatting a PowerPoint document for my horrible boss.'
- ✓ **DO SAY:** 'Delighted to share a great little project I've been working on. Blessed to be part of such an amazing team.'

✗ **DON'T SAY:** 'I'm so bored of my meaningless job I literally re-organised the folders on my desktop today.'

✓ **DO SAY:** 'Thrilled to announce a new organisational classifications system for our digital operability. What a fantastic initiative.'

✗ **DON'T SAY:** 'I gave a five-second update at our WIP meeting today.'

✓ **DO SAY:** 'Honoured to have been invited to give the keynote address at our weekly meeting this morning. #Pinchingmyself.'

✗ **DON'T SAY:** 'I got fired from my last job for incompetence and now the only job available to me is a McDonald's server.'

✓ **DO SAY:** 'Super pumped to announce I'm starting a new role at McDonald's Inc today in an exciting customer-facing role. Can't wait to embark on this new journey.'

LINKEDIN POST GENERATOR

Choose an unnecessarily upbeat adjective

'Excited'
'Delighted'
'Pumped'
'Honoured'
'Stoked'
'Thrilled'

+

'to be'

+

Add a mundane achievement mismatched with gushing descriptor

'Starting a new role with the wonderful <insert role>'
'Joining the super-impressive team at <insert company>'
'Speaking at the world-class <insert event>'
'Launching this amazing new <insert product/brand>'
'Part of this incredible <thing you are part of>'

Finish with a nauseatingly earnest phrase

'Blessed to be part of such an amazing team!'
'Can't wait to see what the next chapter holds!'
'Onwards and upwards!'
'Excited to embark on this new journey.'
'What an exciting next step for the Omo brand!'

EXPERT INSIGHT

'One question I get asked a lot is how personal you should be on LinkedIn. My advice is clear: LinkedIn is a professional environment, so you should only ever talk about your family if you can use them as a prop to drive increased engagement and secure new sales leads.'

Herbert Pierce
LinkedIn Influencer

DON'T SAY:

'I worked the check-out at Tesco.'

DO SAY:

'I managed daily financial transactions at a FTSE 100 company.'

IF WE SPOKE AT HOME LIKE WE SPEAK ON LINKEDIN

'Such a privilege to have been chosen to unstack the dishwasher this morning. So proud to be part of such an inspiring family.'

'Excited to announce that I will be taking out the bins this evening. Would not have been possible without some incredible behind-the-scenes work from the rest of the amazing team at 128 Rushton Street.'

'Delighted to announce new flatmate Chelsea at 3/329 Simpson Avenue. She was previously heading up operations at 11 Broughton Street. Excited to have her on the team.'

'Today is my last day with my husband. Pumped to be starting an exciting new relationship with @RichardWright tomorrow.'

'Happy to share that I have been appointed to pick up the kids from school this afternoon. Can't wait to get started on this exciting project.'

RULE 2 OF LINKEDIN:

Make every minor accomplishment sound like a Nobel Prize-winning achievement

Scroll through LinkedIn and you'd be forgiven for thinking it's an exclusive club for some of the most successful people on Earth. It's not. It's just your mate from high school describing his part-time job at Footlocker as 'Senior, Award-Winning Retail Podiatrist'.

Unfortunately, you're going to need to get in on the wankery, otherwise you'll never be considered for a role ever again. No company will employ someone who has merely worked as a cleaner, when all of the other applicants have had experience as Sanitary Solutions Engineers.

Describing your job on LinkedIn

- ✗ **DON'T SAY:** 'My first job out of uni was taking coffee orders for senior executives.'
- ✓ **DO SAY:** 'I successfully designed and managed a drinks-based ordering and fulfilment program that drove increased productivity outcomes for senior Stakeholders.'

- ✗ **DON'T SAY:** 'I worked the check-out at Tesco Finsbury Park.'
- ✓ **DO SAY:** 'I managed daily financial transactions at an FTSE 100 company.'

Describing achievements on LinkedIn

As well as describing your job on LinkedIn, it's also necessary to post about your achievements.

✗ **DON'T SAY:** 'I started an office footy tipping competition.'
✓ **DO SAY:** 'I combined team-building skills and financial management capabilities to successfully execute a digital-first entertainment initiative.'

✗ **DON'T SAY:** 'I briefly chatted to Jenny in Accounts in the kitchen while I was re-heating a curry for lunch.'
✓ **DO SAY:** 'I am adept at breaking down silos and fostering interdepartmental cohesion.'

✗ **DON'T SAY:** 'I had a scandalous affair with Jenny in Accounts and she got pregnant.'
✓ **DO SAY:** 'I am renowned for building interdepartmental relationships that facilitate cross-pollination.'

The LinkedIn anniversary

One of the other little quirks of LinkedIn is the LinkedIn anniversary. Surely one of the saddest and most pathetic aspects of late-stage capitalism.

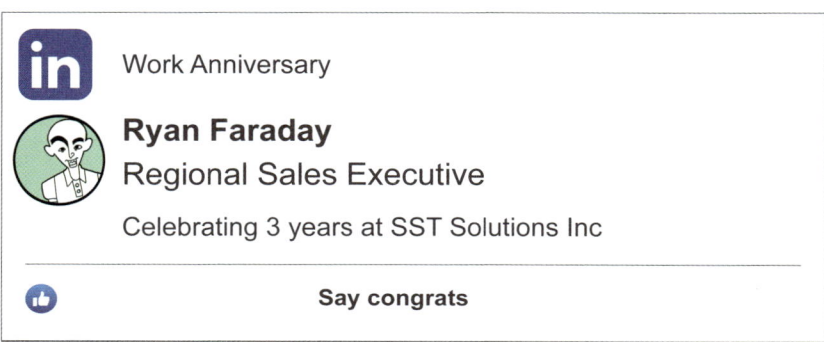

The LinkedIn anniversary post relies on the assumption that people give a shit about how many years you've been working at your current place of employment. But research has shown that people care so little that they would prefer to hear you talk about your dream from last night.

DON'T SAY:

'Stalk.'

DO SAY:

'I'd like to add you to my professional network'

ACTIVITY:
HOW ARISTOTLE USES LINKEDIN

When honing your LinkedIn skills, a great way to practise is to write on behalf of someone else. Pick a celebrity or historical figure and try to summarise their workplace achievements in the LinkedIn style. We've put together some posts and a profile for Aristotle as an example.

 Excited to share that I have just landed a contract for my next book *De Anima*. Still working out the details: I want it to be about the soul and the inadequacies of materialist reductionism, but my publisher wants it to be a recipe book. Either way, I'm aiming to have it on bookshelves by mid-350 BCE. #RecipesByAristotle

 When I founded the Lyceum 10 years ago, we only had one student – a guy named Socrates, who asked too many questions. I told him we'd grow, and we did! By replacing Philosophy with Podcast Studies, we achieved 800% ROI. Congrats to graduate Josiah Roganopolous, whose podcast is Mesopotamia's top-ranked!

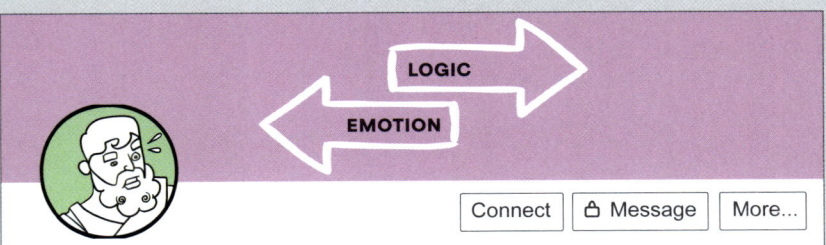

Aristotle

Connect | Message | More...

Thought Disruptor | Knowledge Architect | Inventor of Science

Macedonia

About

Outcomes-focused ethical strategist and influencer with 10+ years experience. As the inventor of logic, I have a proven track record of proving things. Renowned as the 'father of Western thought', I am available for podcast appearances and can speak on a wide variety of topics including logic, metaphysics, mathematics, physics, biology, botany, ethics, politics, agriculture, medicine, dance, and comfortable activewear. (Disclosure: I have an ongoing commercial partnership with Lululemon.)

Highlights

Named 'most influential person in human history' by Agora Weekly, and Man of the Year by Water Clock magazine. Management coach to high-impact leaders, including Alexander of Macedon. Passionate about using categories to organise living things and wearing comfortable activewear.

LinkedIn News

- **Is fire really an element?**
  16h ago
- **Calls for Alexander to suspend campaign ahead of Hyphasis march**
  1d ago
- **Is writing ruining the oral tradition?**
  3d ago
- **Logical reasoning doesn't make sense**
  2w ago

People Also Viewed

Archimedes 2nd
Geometry nerd and bathing enthusiast

Connect

Pythagoras 2nd
Passionate about triangles

Connect

Alexander the Great 2nd
Growth architect

Connect

USING THE WORD 'HUMBLED'

You may have noticed that the word 'humbled' means something a little different when you use it on LinkedIn (or at The Academy Awards).

The Cambridge Dictionary defines humbled as the realisation that you are not as important as you thought you were.

On LinkedIn, humbled is the realisation that you want your followers to think that you are a lot more important than you actually are.

On the opposite page is a typical LinkedIn post that demonstrates the use of the word humbled. Feel free to use it as a template.

 I am humbled to be nominated for this industry award (*that you've never heard of but that sounds impressive*).

I'm not really one to draw attention to these types of things (*which is why I've posted it on a public networking platform used by people I'm trying to impress*).

(*I should probably also mention that*) there are so many talented people in the industry, (*to give the impression that I'm being modest, when actually I'm just letting you know that I'm more talented than them*) so it's an absolute honour to be mentioned in the same breath as these people (*that I fucking despise*)!

Onwards and upwards! (*I have no idea why I added that, but people seem to like that phrase.*)

How to become a LinkedIn influencer

LinkedIn influencers post about their unrealistically perfect working lives to make everyone else feel inferior. It's a bit like being an Instagram influencer, but for ugly people.

If you have low self-esteem and an internet connection (but can't afford botox), becoming a LinkedIn influencer may be for you.

The key is to abandon any regard for self-respect or facts, while also concealing that you have no discernible skills other than self-promotion.

Here are some example posts to get you inspired:

Today I woke up at 3 am, did a 7-hour gym workout followed by a 2-hour yoga class, walked to work, listened to eight motivational podcasts and spent 16 hours working on my business, before coming home to prepare for the evening's triathlon.

That's what true dedication to success looks like.

What's your daily routine?

Today I sacked my whole team so I could post about the experience on LinkedIn and make it all about me. Here's what I learned …

I launched three multi-million-dollar startups before I was thirty. My keys to success?
- Being prepared to put in the work – late nights, early mornings, no weekends
- Backing my intuition and ignoring what the haters say
- Inheriting $20 million
- Creating a great team culture

I bumped into an old colleague yesterday.

We briefly reminisced about our time together at Google.

And then the conversation turned in an unexpected direction.

She asked me, 'How did you turn one hundred LinkedIn followers into one million followers in just two months?'

Here's what I told her.

The key is to hook your reader in by pretending your posts will be interesting.

By the time they realise they're not, it's too late.

They've already been mesmerised by the way you've formatted your post.

With every sentence on a new line.

It makes your posts seem strangely profound.

Intelligent.

Enlightening.

Even when they're not.

EXPERT INSIGHT

'Parenting is basically a competition. So I've always felt it's important to bring your LinkedIn game when describing to your partner the things you have done for your kids. Don't say: I changed Kira's nappy. Do say: I successfully managed the design and deployment of an anti-faecal sanitary initiative that has led to improved client outcomes. I actually used to say that all the time to my wife. Back when we were married.'

Michael Timms
Senior Solutions Architect and Father

END-OF-UNIT QUIZ

Can you guess these jobs from their LinkedIn description?

1. 'I combined my experience in the automotive and logistics sectors to implement end-to-end delivery solutions for a US-based food conglomerate.'
2. 'This LinkedIn profile is provided on the basis that it shall not be copied, facsimiled, or in any other way imitated, notwithstanding any other provision of this Agreement, as set out in clause 5.1.4a.'
3. 'Motivator | Life Coach | Wellness Evangelist'

Answers: 1. Uber Eats Driver 2. Wanker 3. Unemployed

UNIT 8: USING EMAIL

SENDING AND RECEIVING EMAILS IS A CENTRAL PART OF MOST JOBS THESE DAYS. IN MANY ROLES, SENDING EMAILS IS THE ONLY THING YOU'LL DO (APART FROM ATTENDING MEETINGS, WHICH IN MOST CASES COULD HAVE BEEN AN EMAIL ANYWAY).

THE OBJECTIVE OF A WORK EMAIL

~~To communicate effectively with colleagues, customers and other Stakeholders.~~
To maliciously undermine your work colleagues while using an upbeat, pseudo-polite tone.

A lot of people would say that working as a security guard or in a war zone is more combative than working in an office. This is not true. Those people have clearly never had to deal with a passive-aggressive email from a work colleague they hate. *That* is true violence.

Here are some phrases that you'll need to know to successfully navigate your inbox.

PHRASE: 'Nice to e-meet you!'
MEANING: 'I'm trying to numb the pain of my work, which is why I'm talking to you as if you are a child.'

PHRASE: 'I hope this email finds you well.'
MEANING: 'You and your current wellbeing mean nothing to me.'

PHRASE: 'Happy Friday!'
MEANING: 'I am pretending to be nice. I could never be friends with you.'

PHRASE: 'Just checking to make sure you received my email?'
MEANING: 'I know you received my last email. This is just me reminding you to respond by passively aggressively pretending that the delivery mechanism for electronic mail, which has been in place for decades, has inexplicably malfunctioned.'

PHRASE: 'Reattaching for your convenience.'
MEANING: 'Why didn't you open the attachment the first time, you absolute moron?!'

EXPERT INSIGHT

'Email is great, but it's a key vector for phishing attacks by hackers and the leaking of sensitive confidential data. That's why I tell all my clients to always put a large disclaimer at the end of their emails telling people not to use any information inappropriately. That way they're completely safe.'

James Schloeffel

PHRASE: 'Any updates on this?'
MEANING: 'Do your job, shithead!'

PHRASE: 'Just a friendly reminder.'
MEANING: 'I am literally about to rip out your oesophagus with my bare hands.'

PHRASE: 'Just popping this to the top of your inbox.'
MEANING: 'Just mock-politely suggesting you READ YOUR FUCKING EMAILS!'

PHRASE: 'With all due respect.'
MEANING: 'I have absolutely zero respect for you and I am about to outline some very, very specific reasons why.'

PHRASE: 'As per my last email.'
MEANING: 'I hate you and I want you to die.'

PHRASE: 'Copying in Craig.'
MEANING: 'I'm about to get you fired.'

PHRASE: 'Copying in HR.'
MEANING: 'Better get a lawyer, dickhead.'

PHRASE: 'Thanks in advance.'
MEANING: 'You will hate what I've just asked you to do and I don't care.'

PHRASE: 'Best!'
MEANING: 'Die!'

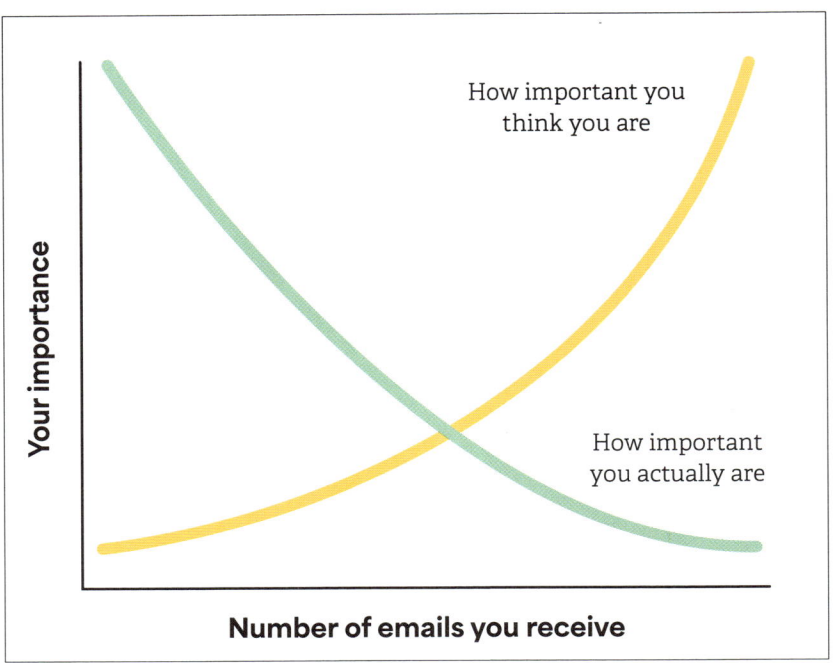

DID YOU KNOW?
The First World War actually started after Franz Ferdinand sent an email to Gavrilo Princip that used the phrase 'as per my last email'. Three days later, Ferdinand was assassinated.

ACTIVITY

Translate the email below into its true meaning.

Hi Viv,
Happy Friday! Just popping this one to the top of your inbox.
Just a friendly reminder that, as per my last email,
I'm hoping to get your slides for the innovation deck by COB today (reattaching for your convenience).
Copying in Craig so he's across this too.
Best,
Brenda

Answer

Hi Viv,
I am pretending to be nice to you but I could never be friends with you!
READ YOUR FUCKING EMAILS!
I am literally about to rip out your oesophagus with my bare hands – I hate you and I want you to die. I'm hoping to get your slides for the innovation deck by COB today (why didn't you open the attachment the first time, you absolute moron?!).
I am about to get you fired.
Die,
Brenda

USING THE REPLY-ALL FUNCTION

From time to time in large organisations, someone will send an email to the entire company to convey some petty gripe about the dishes in the kitchen, which will then trigger hundreds of reply-all emails from other employees, responding to the original email.

These emails will themselves trigger a new round of reply-all emails from angry employees telling the other employees not to use reply-all when they respond because it clogs up their inbox, which will in turn lead to a third round of reply-all emails from separate employees pointing out the irony of people using reply-all to tell people not to use reply-all.

To date, it is not known how to stop these email chains. One email conversation with the subject line 'Whoever jammed the fax machine please fix it', which started in a Sydney office in 1998, is still circulating today in a perpetual reply-all loop.

Scientists are now working on a way to harness the energy created in email chains such as these to solve energy shortages across the world.

EXPERT INSIGHT

'I once consulted for a large fossil fuel company. We conducted a time and motion study that showed that employees were spending an average of two hours and thirty-seven minutes per day answering pointless emails. To solve the problem, we created a checklist of "best practices" that employees were required to follow before they started writing. Within weeks, we'd doubled the amount of time people were spending writing emails. I like to think of it as my contribution to reducing carbon emissions.'

Jason Li
Efficiency Consultant

UNIT 9: HOW TO BE A MANAGER

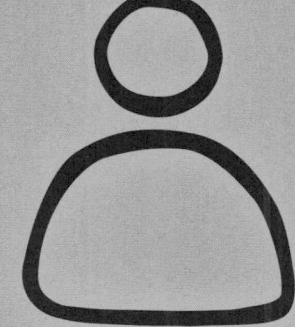

IF YOU'VE MASTERED UNITS 1-8 IN THIS BOOK, YOU'RE READY TO TAKE ON A SENIOR MANAGEMENT POSITION.
IN FACT, YOU'VE PROBABLY ALREADY BEEN PROMOTED.

Management positions are exactly the same as more junior positions, just with more pay and less work.

Here are some tips for navigating your role as a manager.

Always use 'we' when delegating work

As the leader of your team, you'll need to convey to your subordinates that you're all in this together. By using the word 'we' rather than 'you', you can give the impression that you'll be there to help out with the last-minute project late on a Friday afternoon, when of course you'll be down the pub. After all, there's no 'I' in 'team', but there is a 'we' in 'I fucked your weekend'.

- 'Can we get that 15,000 slide presentation done by first thing Monday, Su Yang?'
- 'How are we placed to do an extra three shifts this weekend, Belinda?'

Reward your team for achieving their $14 billion sales target with a $20 gift card

Recognition matters. If your team has been pulling all-nighters to get a new product launched or working weekends to cover staff shortages, make sure you reward them with a small denomination gift card that they'll need to declare for tax purposes.

Celebrate success with a cheap box of pizza

Celebrating success as a team is important, and a free team lunch is a great way to mark any occasion. 'We value your contribution towards achieving an eleven-figure profit margin this year. Here are a dozen $8.99 pizzas from Domino's' is the mantra of many successful managers.

Reframe shit sandwiches as development opportunities

One of the benefits of being a manager is you can delegate to someone else all of the hideously tedious tasks you no longer want to do yourself. The trick is to sell it as a development opportunity.

- ✗ **DON'T SAY:** 'Can you please fill out this 4000-page form that I can't be bothered to do myself?'
- ✓ **DO SAY:** 'Here's a great development opportunity for you as we get closer to your annual review.'

- ✗ **DON'T SAY:** 'Can you please clean the toilet that someone just vomited in?'
- ✓ **DO SAY:** 'There's a development opportunity for you in the third cubicle.'

EXPERT INSIGHT

'Nowadays everyone thinks that you need to get an MBA to be a good manager, but back in the 1980s that wasn't true at all. The main qualification was to have a raging cocaine habit. I miss the 1980s.'

Charles Firth

'In my many years at the bleeding edge of tech, I've learnt that if you say "NFTs are the next big thing" confidently enough, people will forget that you advised them to switch their entire marketing budget to MySpace in 2005.'

Sanushka Kumar
Next Generation Digital Solutionist

Make life-changing conversations sound like casual catch-ups

Being a manager means you have the power to realise, or destroy, another person's dreams in just seconds. Have fun with it!

✗ **DON'T SAY:** 'We need to have a significant, possibly life-changing discussion for which I will provide no context.'
✓ **DO SAY:** 'Quick chat?'

Talk to people as if they're children

Nothing motivates a 52-year-old receptionist more than a phrase such as 'Thanks, Janice! You're a star!'

DON'T SAY:

'You're fired.'

DO SAY:

'Your headcount has been reduced in line with our strategic priorities moving forward.'

EXPERT INSIGHT

'As a Next Generation Digital Solutionist (NGDS), my role is to use imposing-sounding phrases like "If you're not using AI now, your business will not exist in three years" to convince clients to hand over large sums of money for services they could get online for free.'

Jason Hannity
NGDS

HOW TO TELL SOMEONE THEY'RE FIRED

As a manager, it is inevitable from time to time that you will have to fire an employee. But there's no need to use such grotesque, direct language as 'fire'. Here are some other ways to tell someone you are destroying their livelihood.

- 'We're going to have to let you go.'
- 'You have been unassigned to your position.'
- 'There's been a workplace realignment.'
- 'We're undertaking a conscious de-coupling.'
- 'Your role has been right-sized.'
- 'You have been redeployed to a non-working position.'
- 'Your position has been removed from the organisational structure.'
- 'Your headcount has been reduced.'
- 'Due to changing market conditions and a commitment to an innovation-led customer focus, moving forward we have made the mission-critical decision to optimise parts of our people-based team.'
- 'Your employment journey with us has come to an end.'

UNIT 10:
STARTING YOUR OWN CORPO— RATION

SO FAR, WE'VE TAUGHT YOU HOW TO SURVIVE AND THRIVE WHILE WORKING FOR AN EMPLOYER. BUT THERE IS ANOTHER WAY TO MAKE A LIVING, WHICH IS TO START YOUR OWN CORPORATION. IT'S MUCH SIMPLER THAN YOU THINK, PARTICULARLY WHEN YOU CONSIDER THE PURPOSE OF A MODERN CORPORATION IN THE CONTEXT OF WESTERN INDUSTRIALISATION.

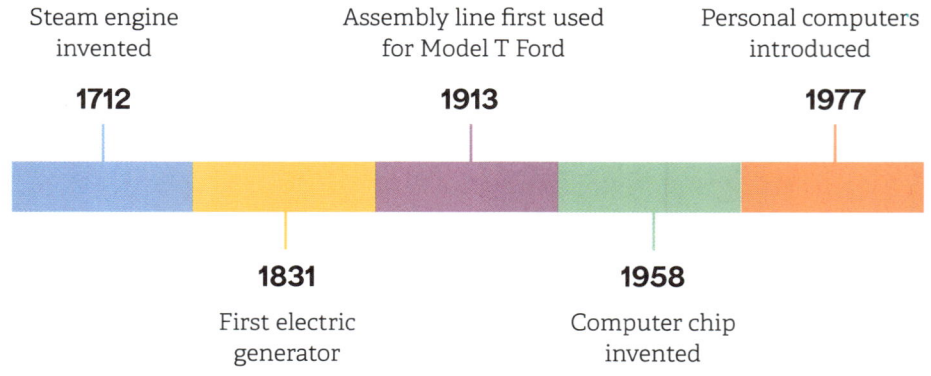

A history of Western industrialisation

The history of Western industrialisation is filled with pivotal moments that forever changed our economy and our way of life. The invention of the steam engine in 1712, Henry Ford's assembly line in 1913, the computer chip in the 1950s and the introduction of online pizza delivery in 1994, all played a major role in improving living standards.

But in the early twenty-first century, after more than 250 years of industrialisation, innovation and progress, a strange thing happened. Companies totally ran out of things to make.

Every conceivable product – from cars and smartphones to takeaway pizza and Dr Pepper-flavoured marshmallows – had already been invented. This was a huge problem, because corporations need to keep producing new things in order to keep growing, and they need to keep growing in order to keep shareholders happy. And shareholders are more important than literally anything else in the world (see page 41).

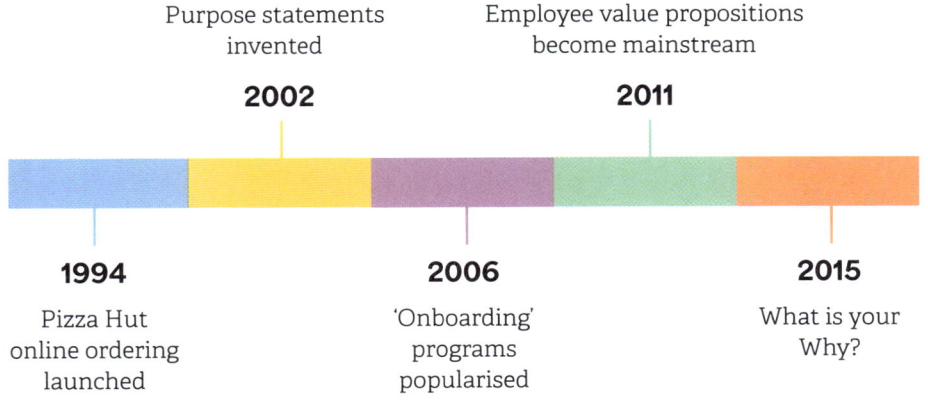

Purpose statements invented
2002

Employee value propositions become mainstream
2011

1994
Pizza Hut online ordering launched

2006
'Onboarding' programs popularised

2015
What is your Why?

Faced with this existential crisis - which threatened not just corporations, but the very existence of capitalism itself - organisations adapted in an ingenious new way. They started producing bullshit. Small amounts of it at first. The odd 'Mission Statement' or 'onboarding program' here. An 'employee value proposition' or 'brand narrative' there. But it soon exploded into the wholesale creation of bullshit - 'Vision Statements' and 'Purpose Statements', '360-degree feedback forms' and entire HR departments.

Instead of developing a new product offering, companies started developing a new set of values. Instead of investing in a new scientific breakthrough, they set up an offsite brainstorming session to define their 'North Star'. They became bullshit-making machines.

 **Instead of developing a new product offering, companies started developing a new set of values.**

Organisations would never again run out of things to make, because there's always an appetite for a new 'customer value proposition' or a 'ways of working manifesto' or, at the very least, an update of one that already exists. Two hundred and fifty years after Adam Smith wrote *The Wealth of Nations*, the problem of scarcity had finally been solved.

Because bullshit is so cheap to make, companies kept producing more and more of it, until, for many corporations, it became their primary product. Some businesses were founded entirely to create bullshit (see Unit 7: LinkedIn, page 169).

At the same time, corporations had to employ more people to produce all of the bullshit, so they started inventing bullshit jobs too. Jobs that had important-sounding titles like 'Special Projects Lead' or 'Marketing Manager', but that involved little more than sitting in meetings all day and saying, 'Let's put a pin in that and circle back later.'*

What's the key takeaway here? It's simply this: if you want to start your own corporation in the twenty-first century, the most essential question is not 'What product will my company make?' or 'What service will it provide?' It's not even 'Who will my target market be?' It is 'What are the five Core Values that will underpin our purpose-led Mission Statement as we seek to align our Vision to our North Star?'

In short, you'll need to become adept at producing bullshit. On the following pages, we step you through how to do exactly that with our patented eight-sided Wankernomics Bullshit Strategy Star Framework Model™ (WBSSFM).

---

* A Senior Data Frameworks System & Processes Analyst Director, Asia Pacific, estimated that around three-quarters of all jobs are primarily concerned with creating bullshit.

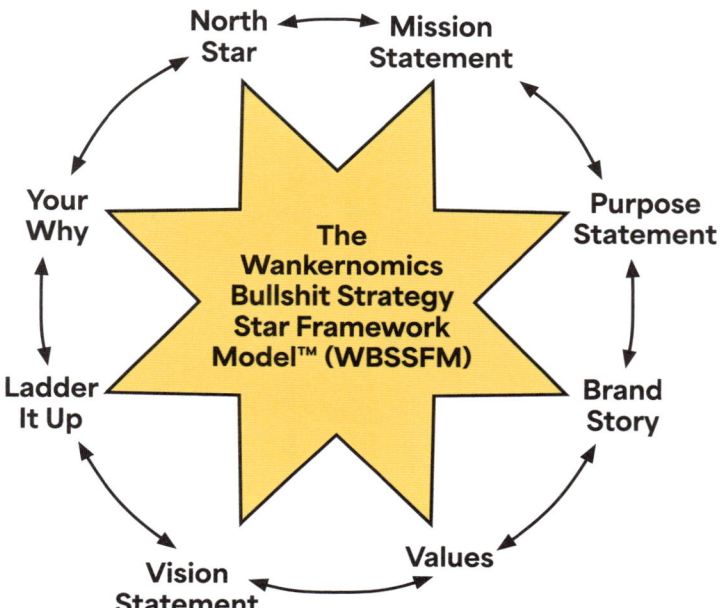

STEP 1:

Define your 'Why'

As an employee, you've no doubt sought to define your 'why' many times before. 'Why the fuck am I here?', 'Why do I get paid less than Graham when he has the intellectual heft of a toddler?' and 'Why did I accidentally just call my boss "Mum" in this morning's meeting FML!'

For answers to those questions, you'll need to refer to page 10, page 16 and your therapist.

But if you're in charge of a company, your 'Why' is something altogether different – an absolutely crucial piece of grandiose-sounding bullshit that you can talk about endlessly at conferences, in blog posts and on LinkedIn.

A bit like your North Star on page 220 (actually, exactly like your North Star on page 220), your Why is a statement that describes what you want other people to think drives every decision in your business.

The trick is to come up with an elaborate phrase that makes it sound like your organisation exists for some reason entirely different than the obvious one, which is to make lots of money.

Spotify's Why, for example, isn't to 'To achieve super profits through the use of a near-monopoly platform that exploits musicians by paying them virtually nothing.' It isn't even 'To allow people to access millions of songs.' No, Spotify's Why is 'To unlock the potential of human creativity.' Because before Spotify, human imagination and artistic endeavour were inaccessible. It was waiting for an audio streaming company

to come along with a key and finally unlock its potential.

Hemingway, Austen and Dickens all endured writer's block for months on end simply because they couldn't tap into the back catalogue of their favourite artist and unleash years of pent-up creativity. Van Gogh would sit at his easel, bereft of inspiration, thinking, if only there was a song streaming service that I could access on a monthly plan.

Spotify's Why, like all company Whys, is said to be the driving force behind every decision the company makes.

The reason they raised their monthly fees again? Because it makes them enormous amounts of money? No, you idiot. It's because it unlocks the potential of human creativity.

The reason they choose to pay artists just 0.3 cents per stream? Because it increases their profitability? Don't be so cynical. It's because it unlocks the potential of human creativity.

Hopefully you're getting the hang of how this all works.

How to define your Why

Your Why is a pretentious phrase that provides a socially acceptable reason for your company's existence. Ideally, it should be formulated only after an all-day workshop with staff involving break-out groups, flip charts and colourful pens. But if you haven't got time for that, a handy shortcut is to choose a random inspirational quote from Barack Obama. No-one will ever know the difference.

We've prepared a list of Obama quotes for you to choose from. Any one will do.

- 'Making sure that the world we leave our children is just a little bit better than the one we inhabit today.'
- 'To come together to save this planet.'
- 'To be the change that we seek.'
- 'To fill the world with hope.'
- 'Why can't I just eat my waffle?'
- 'To not leave our children a world where the oceans rise and famine spreads.'
- 'To have the chance to make our lives what we will.'
- 'To believe that there are better days ahead.'
- 'I miss Saturday morning. Rolling out of bed, not shaving.'
- 'To have the courage to keep reaching, to keep working, to keep fighting.'
- 'The thing about hip-hop today is it's smart, it's insightful. The way they can communicate a complex message in a very short space is remarkable.'

STEP 2:

Create your North Star

Your company's 'North Star' is your unwavering reference point that guides you in everything you do. Or, more realistically (and in accordance with the metaphor), a small shiny thing off in the distance that you'll never actually reach and that is technically already dead.

The North Star is most famous for guiding the three wise men in Biblical times. They didn't find organisational growth at the end of their journey, of course; they found a baby shower in a cow shed. So maybe as a business metaphor, it's not ideal.

Nevertheless, it is a term that is used more and more these days. The fact that it is impossible to see the North Star in the southern hemisphere has not stopped wankers in Australia

and New Zealand adopting the term. 'We use our North Star to guide all of our critical decisions' takes on new meaning when you realise you can't actually see the fucking thing. Although, granted, it's probably better than saying you have an 'Organisation Southern Cross', which would kick off a culture war that no-one has the time for right now.

Put simply, a North Star is another piece of manufactured bullshit that can be used to justify an external consultant and an offsite workshop for middle management.

How to create your North Star

1. On a piece of paper, write down a list of clearly articulated things you'd like to achieve in your business.
2. Throw away the piece of paper.
3. Write down whatever you came up with for your Why (see page 219).

My company's North Star is

_____.

STEP 3:

Develop your Mission Statement

Your Mission Statement describes the reason your organisation exists. Which sounds eerily similar to your North Star and your Why, but please don't think too deeply about this because the careers of millions of marketers, strategists and consultants are depending on you not concluding that it's all useless.

And anyway, as we said at the start of this chapter, the entire economic system is now propped up by the ongoing production of bullshit, which means that not having a Mission Statement could ultimately cause the collapse of capitalism.

How to develop your Mission Statement

Developing a Mission Statement is very straightforward. You simply need to write down the words 'To put our customers at the centre of everything we do'. (You can sub out the word 'centre' for 'core' or 'heart' if you're feeling disruptive and you want to shake things up a little.)

Go to the website of any large company (and we mean *any*), put the words 'customers' and 'everything we do' into the search bar and we guarantee you will find the phrase 'Our customers are at the centre of everything we do' or something very similar.

THE WANKERNOMICS LOGO

'The result of an $8.2-million design process, the Wankernomics logo represents a brave new direction for our brand.

It is a marque that is both modern yet timeless; sophisticated yet stylish; orange, but also a bit yellow. Acting as a catalyst for conversation and curiosity, the new logo evokes deep feelings of connectedness, community and innovation, while also conveying our mission of creating betterer solutions for tomorrow's future, today, together. Astute viewers may also detect a subtle "W" shape. It stands for "Wankernomics".

We're excited by the new logo. And we can't wait to roll it out across all of our touchpoints.

In the meantime, we are developing a 3000-page style guide to ensure the correct usage of the logo.'

- JAMES SCHLOEFFEL, CHIEF DISRUPTOR & OPTIMISATION-SOLUTION STRATEGIST AT WANKERNOMICS: THRIVING FOR BETTERER

WANKERNOMICS TRANSLATOR

PHRASE:

'DISRUPTOR'
[pronounce: tax-cheat]

↓

MEANING:

'A company that replicates what another business has done successfully for decades, but without paying any tax.'

STEP 4:

Define your Purpose Statement

A Purpose Statement is the who, how, what and when of your organisation. It's a lot like your Brand Story (see page 228), just with fewer words.

Our Purpose Statement Generator™ is a simple tool you can use to piece together random phrases. Here we've shown how the Purpose Statement Generator™ would work for a small dental practice, but it can work for any organisation.

Purpose Statement Generator™
Pick one phrase from each of the sections below.

Part 1: WHAT your company does
Resist the urge to write something explanatory here like 'Provides dental services'; that is massively lacking in ambition. It needs to be incomprehensibly large-scale. Here are some choices:

a. Creating a better planet
b. Bringing communities together
c. Reimagining dentistry
d. Unleashing the power of next.

Part 2: HOW your company does it
You're probably immediately reaching for phrases like 'Using

dental drills and fluoride paste'. But that's way too specific. Instead choose from one of these much loftier sounding solution-led phrases:
a. Providing innovative solutions
b. Providing integrated solutions
c. Providing world-class solutions
d. Providing human-centric solutions.

Part 3: WHO your company does it for
If you're new to this, you might think the answer to this question is 'People who need to see a dentist in Croydon'. Wrong. Think bigger:
a. All of humanity
b. The planet
c. People just like you
d. Communities large and small.

Part 4: WHAT they will get out of it
You've probably guessed by now that it's a lot more than just getting a check-up and a clean:
a. Thrive
b. Enjoy a better future
c. Be their best selves
d. Feel connected to something bigger.

Part 5: WHEN this will happen
While putting a specific completion date on your client's filling would be useful, you want something much less meaningful:
a. Today and tomorrow

b. For generations to come
c. Until every tooth has a chance to live a brighter tomorrow
d. One tooth at a time.

Part 6: WEIRD bit at the end

There will always be some leftover words from your brainstorming session that don't fit neatly elsewhere. Just pop them at the end (choose as many as necessary):
a. At scale
b. Together
c. Collaboratively
d. In an ever-changing world.

Putting it all together

At <name of company> we are <PART 1 selection> by <PART 2 selection> so that <PART 3 selection> can <PART 4 selection> <PART 5 selection>, <PART 6 selections>.

Example:

At **Croydon Dentistry** we are **reimagining dentistry** by **providing human-centric solutions** so that **communities large and small** can **thrive for generations to come, at scale, together in an ever-changing world**.

STEP 5:

Write your Brand Story

Your Brand Story (or Brand Narrative) is an inspiring piece of writing that describes the many ways a large multinational organisation is changing the world for the better. It has no relationship with reality.

A Brand Story is an imaginary world where large corporations 'bring communities together' through 'innovation', 'imagination' and a commitment to 'doing what's right' so that everyone can 'prosper', 'thrive' and 'be their authentic selves' in an 'ever-changing world'.

Ordinary things are 're-invented', 'revolutionised' and 're-imagined'. Problems are 'tackled'; challenges are 'embraced'. All in the name of 'a better tomorrow, today'. 'Together.'

Read one of these things and you'd be forgiven for thinking that it was describing a cure for aging, not an insurance conglomerate.

How to write your Brand Story

Here are some key words and phrases you'll need to use to write an inspirational Brand Story.

1. 'Community'

Whether you're a multi-billion-dollar hedge fund or a global arms manufacturer, it's essential to give the impression that you are a wholesome, neighbourhood-run collective that's part of the tapestry of the local community.

You can never use the word 'community' too much. You're in touch with it, you're focused on it, you're bringing it together, and most importantly, you're an integral part of it. Until, of course, you are sued for ripping apart the very fabric of it, in which case you are headquartered in the Cayman Islands for legal and taxation purposes.

2. 'We're creating a better world'

Workplaces are filled with enthusiastic, idealistic Millennials and Gen Z-ers who, as children, dreamed of working for the United Nations, not a bathroom supplies wholesaler. So it's essential to indulge their delusion by telling them that your company is focused on changing the world, one faucet at a time.

Never mind that a bathroom wholesaler that services the southern suburbs of Perth has limited capacity to create a better suburb, let alone a better world. Don't let that stop you dreaming big.

3. 'Tomorrow'

While most human beings are concerned with what they're going to cook for dinner tonight or getting Liam to put on his fucking socks and shoes, if you're a large corporation it is essential that you are concerned only with 'tomorrow'. It's a nebulous concept that doesn't actually mean 24 hours from now, but rather some undefined point in the future.

In your Brand Story (as well as on any TV commercials and online communications) you should make it clear that your organisation is not just creating a better tomorrow, but also a brighter tomorrow, a more prosperous tomorrow, a tomorrow that everyone can share in, a tomorrow in which we can all thrive and a tomorrow that doesn't cost the earth. Critically, you need to be doing all of this TODAY. For example, 'We're creating a better tomorrow for everyone, today.'

As deadlines go, the ambiguous definition of 'tomorrow' is kind of brilliant, because it never actually arrives. As long as you claim that you are working towards tomorrow, today, you never actually have to do anything.

💬 **CUSTOMER COMPLAINT:** You said fourteen years ago you were creating a brighter tomorrow.

💬 **YOUR RESPONSE:** We are!

4. 'Together'

In reality, your customers are nothing more than an annoying but necessary requirement for profit-making that you try to keep at arm's length. But in your communications, you need to give the impression that you involve them in everything, as if your company is just one big community working bee.

#WANKERNOMICSINSPO

'Have you touched someone's base today?'

- **GOOD:** Let's create a better tomorrow.
- **BETTER:** Let's create a better tomorrow, today.
- **BEST:** Let's create a better tomorrow, today. Together.

Be sure to include some of these phrases in your Brand Story.
- 'Together we can create a better world.'
- 'When we work together, anything is possible.'
- 'Working together for a more connected community.'
- 'Moving forward together for a better tomorrow, today.'

5. 'At the heart of everything we do'

If you've read the Develop your Mission Statement section of this unit (page 222), you'll know that your customers are at the centre (or core, or heart) of everything you do. But that doesn't mean everything else can't also be at the centre (or core, or heart).

Read the website of any bank, insurance company or retail conglomerate and you'll soon discover that sustainability, people, inclusion, diversity, innovation, Key Stakeholders and communities are also at the centre of everything they do, all at once.

It's a magical, multi-dimensional world where everything and everyone is your number one priority simultaneously.

6. 'The world is changing faster than ever before'

Putting aside the fact that life probably changed pretty fast for Polish people when Germany invaded in 1939, or for Aboriginal people when a dozen boats arrived in Sydney Harbour in 1788, or for humans in general when they discovered how to harness fire for the first time 700,000 years ago, in the realm of brand stories and marketing speak, it is an irrefutable fact that life has never changed faster than it's changing right now.

Use this phrase, then reassure your readers that you'll help them navigate this terrifying, ever-changing world with an everyday saver account, or whatever futile thing you're selling.

STARTING A LARGE CORPORATION NOT FOR YOU?

If you'd prefer to run a smaller company, just be sure to use the word 'boutique' when you describe it.

- ✗ **DON'T SAY:** 'I got sacked from my finance job, so I started up my own consultancy, but it's not going so well and I've only got one client.'
- ✓ **DO SAY:** 'We're a boutique financial services firm offering dedicated, tailored solutions to a hand-picked suite of clients.'

INSPIRATIONAL BUSINESS QUOTES

'Getting promoted at work is the most important thing you can do with your life.' - NELSON MANDELA

'Creativity is not negotiable. It's the only thing that matters.'
- STEVE JOBS (ON CHOOSING AN ACCOUNTANT)

'It is better to be rich than happy, but ideally you'd be both, I reckon.' - THE DALAI LAMA

'Work is a ladder that you can walk up and down, but never side to side.' - JOE (MY PAINTER)

STEP 6:

Define your Values

Company Values are a set of four or five virtuous-sounding words that allow large corporations to say 'We're a Values-led organisation' while they continue to underpay their employees and cut down old-growth rainforests.

A company's Values are designed as the key morals that guide the behaviour of every single person within the organisation. This can be a little tricky if the company employs 20,000+ people from different backgrounds and cultures, and particularly when it also 'celebrates inclusion and diversity' and encourages employees to 'Bring Their Whole Self to Work' (see page 102).

So to keep everyone happy, Values generally end up being a list of bland words describing the bare minimum level of acceptable human behaviour, with a few other fun words like 'Curious' thrown in for good measure.

How to define your Values

Formulating a company's Values is usually a six-month process that involves around 3000 hours of senior management time, 1000 packets of Post-it notes and half a million dollars in consulting fees. But we've formulated a short-cut method that takes around 3 minutes, costs nothing and achieves the same outcome.

Stage 1: Pick one word from each of the five categories below

Words that describe bare minimum decent human behaviour
- Care
- Do the right thing
- Honesty
- Integrity
- Respect

Things we wish we were but are not
- Courageous/bold
- Creative
- Committed to excellence
- Fun!
- Innovative
- Passionate

HR told us to put these in
- Diversity
- Inclusive

A consulting firm told us to put these in
- Collaborative
- Commitment
- Curious

Fuck, we almost forgot customers!
- Customers

#WANKERNOMICSINSPO

'Always ensure you have your low-hanging mixed metaphors lined up on the same hymn sheet.'

UNIT 10: STARTING YOUR OWN CORPORATION

Stage 2: Hold a company-wide launch event to unveil the new Values to employees

And massively misjudge their enthusiasm for incorporating five unrelated words into their daily work life.

At the launch event, ensure you present the Values with a baffling level of excitement, as if you've just revealed a 200 per cent salary raise for all staff, and not the words 'Respectful', 'Collaborative', 'Inclusive' and 'Bold'. (If your Values happen to all start with the same letter – e.g. Customer, Courage, Commitment, Care – be sure to express extra delight about how clever the whole thing is.)

Give everyone a little gift (a tote bag or lollipop, for example) with the new Values written on them – grown adults love this type of thing – and tell them to 'Live the Values'.

Stage 3: Put your chosen Values on your company website

Be sure to include the phrase 'Our Values are at the centre of everything we do'.

Stage 4: Continue underpaying your employees/price gouging your customers/ruining the environment/undermining the fabric of society (choose as appropriate)

No-one needs to know your Values are not actually meaningful drivers of behaviour but, rather, just a few words you put on a website to make you look good.

How Values work in practice

It's easy to assume that a company's Values are nothing more than a few empty words that have no bearing on a company's actions. But if you look into the details, you'll discover that's absolutely true.

For the most part, your Values will just sit on a poster in the office kitchen, next to the 'YOUR MUM DOESN'T WORK HERE' sign, and never serve any purpose.

But there are a few occasions when they'll come in handy.

1. To trick prospective Gen Z graduates into believing they'll be working for a wholesome, purpose-led organisation.
2. To distance yourself from a sports star you sponsor who has done something problematic. For example, 'Our former client's social media post supporting the workplace practices of Joseph Stalin does not align with our company values.'
3. To provide your CEO with some words to say during a Royal Commission.

EXPERT INSIGHT

> 'Large brands usually measure their advertising impact not on sales but on their percentage of "mind share". The idea is that humans are bombarded with 6000 brand impressions every day. Therefore, for Coca-Cola to be the most front-of mind brand in the world, they need to get as many brand impressions as possible. That's why they paid me to mention them in this book.'
>
> James Schloeffel

WANKERNOMICS TRANSLATOR

PHRASE:

'We are a values-led organisation.'

MEANING:

'We did an offsite brainstorm session with an external consultant last year where we wrote down the words 'honesty', 'inclusion' and another one I can't remember right now and then pinned a print-out up in the office kitchen.'

STEP 7:

Develop your Vision Statement

Like your North Star, Purpose Statement and Mission Statement, your Vision Statement describes what you would like other people to think you want your organisation to achieve.

Honestly, by this point it's probably easiest just to copy and paste your Mission or Purpose Statement and change a few words.

STEP 8:

Ladder it up

Once you've finished developing your Why, North Star, Mission Statement, Purpose Statement, Brand Story, Values and Vision Statement, you'll need to put them all together in a ridiculously complex diagram that shows how everything 'ladders up' (which basically just means 'fits together' but sounds better).

Senior executives in large organisations will spend weeks connecting everything together and 'joining the dots' in these elaborate charts, only to present it publicly and discover that no-one gives a shit.

Nevertheless, this chart will become incredibly powerful in your organisation. Any suggestion made by anyone in the organisation, no matter how useful, can be shot down forever with the phrase, 'It doesn't ladder up to the overarching single source of truth.'

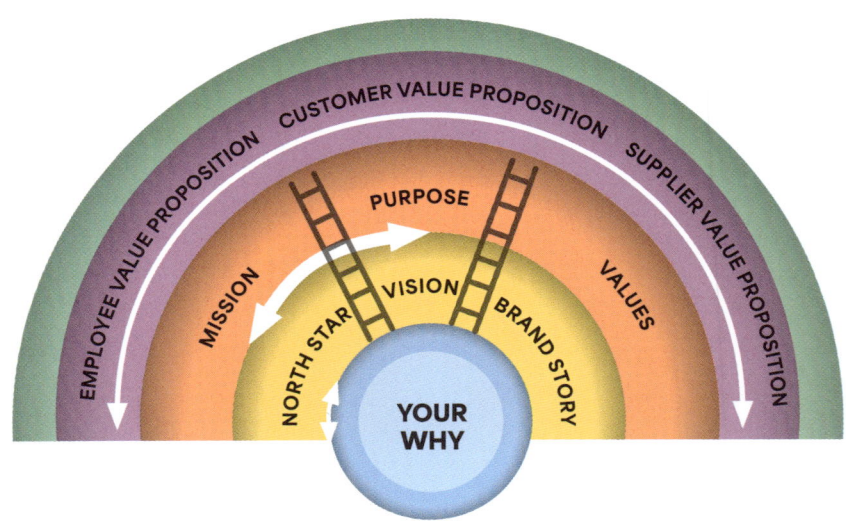

Business communications

Developing your Why, North Star, Mission, Purpose, Brand Story, Values and Vision, and then ensuring that they ladder up, will only take 2-3 years. Although keep in mind that they will need to be updated every 1-2 years, and more frequently if a new CEO or CMO joins the business.

In the spare time in between, you can start to promote your business to the general public. Here are a few different words and phrases to help you get started.

Use the word 'solution'

The Oxford Dictionary defines a solution as 'a means of solving a problem or dealing with a difficult situation'. But in the business world it can mean basically anything you want it to. Most commonly, it's used to add a false sense of sophistication and complexity to an otherwise straightforward service offering.

Consider the comparative hourly rates of the tradesperson who says, 'I am a plumber', and the one who says, 'I provide plumbing solutions', and you'll start to understand the value of using this word.

The two plumbers offer identical services, of course, but only one gives the impression that they are executing a complex installation of critical hardware, rather than replacing a downpipe.

You'll notice too that the word is usually used in its plural form, 'solutions', to cleverly give the impression that the business in question has more than one trick up its sleeve, when they almost certainly don't.

You can be pretty certain that Alpha Painting Solutions has only one method for painting your house. And, if you were to ask Joe's Gardening Solutions to give you a quote for pruning your hedge, and then ask them to quote again, but this time using one of their other gardening solutions, it's pretty likely Joe will look at you as if you have lost the plot.

Innovative solutions for using the word solutions

In most cases, 'solutions' is paired with a service offering (Catering Solutions, Building Solutions, Design Solutions, etc.). But it is possible to go a step further, forgoing any attempt to provide context or meaning at all.

For example, if you want to start your own business but you don't have any services to offer, just say 'We provide innovative solutions' and you're on your way to securing your first customer. Add a few other empty phrases, slap up a website and develop a meaningless Purpose Statement (see page 225), and you'll be ready to list on the stock market.

Thousands of successful businesses are based on nothing more than an overconfident founder and a website that says 'We provide innovative solutions to meet your bespoke needs in a fast-paced, ever-changing world'.

Bored of saying 'Innovative solutions'? Try these incredibly different alternatives:

- state-of-the-art solutions
- bespoke solutions
- tailored solutions
- best-in-class solutions
- best-of-breed solutions.

✗ **DON'T SAY:** 'We fill out tax returns.'
✓ **DO SAY:** 'At Abacus Accounting, we provide innovative accounting solutions.'

Be sure to deliver outcomes

Outcomes are basically the same as solutions, except they're for government and not-for-profit organisations.

Where a website design company might provide 'Innovative solutions for our clients', a government department will provide 'Better outcomes for our communities'.

There are many different outcomes your organisation can provide: Learning Outcomes, Community Outcomes, Stakeholder Outcomes, Health Outcomes, Educational Outcomes and just Outcomes. Choose the ones that feel right for you.

There is no need to define what those outcomes might be, just that they'll be 'better', 'enhanced' or 'improved'.

This saves you a lot of time that would otherwise be wasted trying to define what it is you actually plan to achieve.

One final point. It's not good enough to just attain or complete outcomes, you'll need to deliver them – as if you're a postal service popping outcomes into a letterbox.

✗ **DON'T SAY:** 'We haven't had time to create a coherent plan about what we're actually doing because we spent three months developing a Mission Statement.'
✓ **DO SAY:** 'We're delivering better community outcomes for everyone.'

COMMS STOCK FOOTAGE CHECKLIST

Have you included these must-have images in your advertisement or corporate video?

- wind turbines
- fields of solar panels
- people walking along a beach, preferably wearing white linen, ideally with at least one child on a man's shoulders
- people sitting around a table laughing while a woman places an entire chicken or turkey in the centre
- a dog with a roll of toilet paper
- a science lab
- a bizarre animation of atoms and enzymes (for cleaning products).

Always take a holistic, end-to-end approach

Whether you're talking about a solution, a system, a framework or an approach, it's essential that it's holistic and preferably end-to-end as well. No-one wants half a solution. Yuck!

✗ **DON'T SAY:** 'We design brochures.'
✓ **DO SAY:** 'We offer end-to-end, holistic design solutions.'

Always add value (AAV)

We explained the value of adding value as an employee on page 44, but adding value is also a great value-add if you're running a business. By using the term, you avoid the need to define what you actually offer your customers.

'We offer value-added solutions to customers in markets across the globe' is an entirely acceptable, utterly meaningless way to describe your business on your About Us page.

Achieving diversity (of stock footage)

These days it's not socially viable to run a large corporation without proper representation of minority groups in your stock footage.

While it may be true that the vast majority of your senior positions are filled by middle-aged white men, it's vital that you be one hundred per cent committed to promoting young dark-skinned women wearing hard hats to the front page of your company's website.

DON'T SAY:

'This logo is a black circle.'

DO SAY:

'This brand identity evokes a sense of openness and warmth, while expressing the interconnectedness of the brand to its people, its customers and its communities. Its simplicity betrays a hidden complexity – cleverly embodying the multi-layered nature of the brand and its ongoing narrative within this space. It cost $20 million.'

Doing a sports tie-in?

If you're making an advertisement to tie in with football coverage, be sure to include a group of people looking at a TV screen wearing an array of different team jerseys and scarfs and holding a football, while eating perfectly placed, oversized bowls of chips, exactly like the way no-one ever watches football.

Developing your logo

There are many different ways to develop your logo, but ideally it should cost you eight times what you thought it would, have a 4000-word accompanying document that uses words like 'evokes', 'symbolises' and 'conjures', and ultimately look like a circle drawn by a small child.

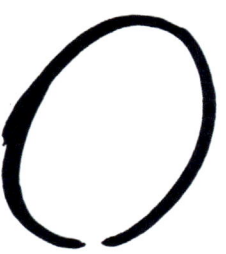

This logo for an insurance brand cost $20 million to create.

NEXT STEPS

CONGRATULATIONS. YOU'VE FINISHED READING A BOOK.

If you've properly applied these strategies, you should already be well on your way to leading a large multinational organisation.

More importantly, you now have the opportunity to smugly broadcast your discovery of this exciting new book to your colleagues, thereby increasing your professional status, as well as our sales figures.

Here are five things you can do straight away:

1. Post this exact statement on Linkedin: 'Delighted to announce that I've just finished reading a brilliant new book called *Wankernomics* that outlines the best-practice strategies for achieving success in an ever-changing working world. Buy it! #lifechanging #success #wankernomics'
2. Set up a recurring weekly meeting at your workplace to discuss the key takeaways from this book.
3. Send an all-staff email that expects to find people well, and reattaches the details of how to buy this book for their convenience.
4. Convert this book into a 450-slide PowerPoint deck and deliver it as a tedious four-hour workshop. Give everyone who attends a copy of the book.
5. Run an ideation session with your team to develop innovative new strategies for telling people that you've read this book. Socialise your outputs with your colleagues.

That's it! All that's left to do now is fill in the feedback form.

FEEDBACK FORM

1. On a scale of 1 to 5 how likely are you to fill in this form?

2. What about if we showed you some smiley faces?

3. What are the things that you like about this form?

4. What are the other things you like about this form?

5. Do you find it annoying when a form makes a question compulsory for no discernible reason? Please explain why/why not (compulsory).

6. Please write a 500-word essay on a topic of your choice.

Are there any ways this form could be improved? ☐ N

ABOUT THE AUTHORS

James and Charles are two of the country's most accomplished comedy writers and performers, known for their unique brand of biting satire and observational comedy.

James is the founder of satirical website *The Shovel*, and previously worked in (and somehow survived) the corporate world. Charles is co-founder of The Chaser and co-host of *The Chaser Report*.

They founded Wankernomics in 2023 as a way to help ordinary people navigate the modern workplace, and as a way for James to work through his unresolved issues.

For details of upcoming Wankernomics live shows, visit Wankernomics.com.

For more tips and tricks for surviving workplace hell, follow Wankernomics on social media (@Wankernomics).

JAMES SCHLOEFFEL worked for more than a decade in the corporate world as a marketing manager, copywriter and 'brand voice consultant', so he knows a thing or two about being a wanker.

In 2012 James started *The Shovel*, an influential Australian satirical website that has been referred to in Parliament, Senate Estimates, *The Economist* and, most notably, *Insight English Skills Year 9, Queensland Edition*.

James's writing has also been published in *The Guardian*, *The Sydney Morning Herald*, *The Australian Financial Review* and *The Independent*.

He is based in Melbourne. He also lives in Melbourne.

CHARLES FIRTH is a co-founder of the Australian satirical comedy group The Chaser, and has worked in television, radio and publishing for 25 years. He is author of the bestselling book *American Hoax* and co-creator of *Optics* (ABC TV). In 2024, Charles uploaded his brain into an AI chatbot, and is now able to be downloaded onto your phone using the CharlesGPT app.

Published in 2025 by Hardie Grant Books,
an imprint of Hardie Grant Publishing

Hardie Grant Books (Melbourne)
Wurundjeri Country
Level 11, 36 Wellington Street
Collingwood, Victoria 3066

Hardie Grant North America
2912 Telegraph Ave
Berkeley, California 94705

hardiegrant.com/books

Hardie Grant acknowledges the Traditional Owners of the Country on which we work, the Wurundjeri People of the Kulin Nation and the Gadigal People of the Eora Nation, and recognises their continuing connection to the land, waters and culture. We pay our respects to their Elders past and present.

All rights reserved. No part of this publication may be reproduced, stored in a retrieval system or transmitted in any form by any means, electronic, mechanical, photocopying, recording or otherwise, without the prior written permission of the publishers and copyright holders.

The moral rights of the authors have been asserted.

Copyright text © James Schloeffel & Charles Firth 2025
Copyright illustrations © Matt Taylor 2025
Copyright design © Hardie Grant Publishing 2025

A catalogue record for this book is available from the National Library of Australia

Wankernomics
ISBN 978 1 76145 151 5
ISBN 978 1 76144 261 2 (ebook)

10 9 8 7 6 5 4 3 2 1

Publishing Director: Pam Brewster
Head of Editorial: Jasmin Chua
Project Editor: Ana Jacobsen
Editor: Martine Lleonart
Creative Director: Kristin Thomas
Designer: Kate Barraclough
Head of Production: Todd Rechner
Production Controller: Jessica Harvie
Illustrator: Matt Taylor
Design consultant: Bettina Tan

Colour reproduction by Splitting Image Colour Studio
Printed in China by Leo Paper Products LTD.

The paper this book is printed on is from FSC®-certified forests and other sources. FSC® promotes environmentally responsible, socially beneficial and economically viable management of the world's forests.